GENERATION TO GENERATION

*The Story of the
Church Council of
Greater Seattle*

1919-1995

PANPRESS

For Information Contact:

 PANPRESS, PUBLISHERS
3430 PACIFIC AVENUE, SE
SUITE A-6, BOX #154
OLYMPIA, WA 98501

Cover design by Tamara Broadhead
Illustration by Victor Steinbrueck, courtesy of the
    Seattle Post-Intellingencer
Top photo courtesy of *The Seattle Times*
Lower photo courtesy of *The Source*
    Both photos are from the Special Collections Division
    of the University of Washington Libraries
    (#UW16555 and #UW16551)

Published in United States of America

For Additional Copies contact:

Church Council of Greater Seattle
4759 15th Avenue N.E.
Seattle, Washington 98105
Phone: (206) 525-1213
Fax: (206) 525-1218

Contents

Dedication

The Rev. Gertrude Louise Apel, D.D.

November 7, 1896 – March 15, 1966

Born and brought up on farms in southwestern and central Minnesota, from early childhood, long before her denomination authorized women clergy, Gertrude Louise Apel aspired to be a Methodist minister. In preparation she attended college and seminary in Chicago. During the next forty-six years she had at least five types of ministerial careers.

Her first two years (1918-1920) were spent in rural northeast Montana as a young missionary. Then, for the next eight years (1920-1928), she was a circuit-riding pastor in the Methow Valley and Chewelah, Washington. Completing her apprenticeship as it were, she was Christian education director and associate pastor of the new Trinity Methodist Church in northwest Seattle (1929-1930).

Her fourth career and her major life work, spanning the years 1930-1958, was ecumenical. As General Secretary, she forged the Washington-Northern and Seattle Councils of Churches and Christian Education into one of the most noteworthy ecumenical agencies (for they functioned as one) in the nation, and in the process brought much honor and recognition to herself and the work she was leading. It is quite probable that she was the *first* woman, and for quite a while, the *only* woman to head up a strong state/metropolitan interchurch body.

In her concluding years (1959-1966) she undertook her fifth career as founding pastor of the suburban Marine View Methodist Church in Federal Way, lying between Seattle and Tacoma.

Many have left testimony that she was endowed with liberal dashes of speaking prowess, faith, poise, good judgment, tact, common sense, a magnetic personality, sincerity, courage, humor and wit, broad sympathy and understanding of others, readiness to answer any call of need, talent to impart her zeal and enthusiasm to others, leadership style, organizational genius, charisma with young people (as well as adults), and ability to relate well to the male-dominated church, governmental, and community structures of her time.

She combined an interesting mix of practical skills:

- *some of which were traditionally feminine,* such as music and art;
- *some that had been too often denied to women* but in which she excelled, such as hiking and fishing;
- and *some, which from time immemorial had been strictly masculine*, such as electrical work—so that after passing her Underwriter's test 100 per cent, based on self-study and observation, she was able to wire her grandmother's house as well as two of her churches. Skilled also in woodcraft and carving, she was able to swing a hammer, help church building projects, and in her last parish to build the church altar.

Dr. Apel was an unusual figure in the church of her times. Well before the Methodist church officially enabled women to become clergy, she was licensed to preach (1920). She was one of two women in her denomination to be the first to be ordained—on the same day in 1926. In the 1930s, 1940s, 1950s, and 1960s, to use a tired phrase, she was a "mover and shaker" not only in Seattle, but also in Olympia as well as central and eastern Washington. In the course of her years she became a nationally recognized church leader. High regard came in many ways, including, in 1949, being the first woman to be elected president of the Association of Council Secretaries (the national body of her ecumenical peers), and, in 1950, the first woman to be awarded an honorary degree by the University of Puget Sound.

This historical account of the Church Council of Greater Seattle is dedicated to one who may well be regarded as a "foremother" in the faith. Her memory should not soon fade away.

(Taken in part from the first of a series of articles celebrating Dr. Apel's centennial, published January, 1996, in The Source, *monthly newspaper of the Church Council of Greater Seattle. Those who wish further information about Dr. Apel should consult these articles.)*

Acknowledgments

The Church Council of Greater Seattle has had through the years the enormous devotion of thousands of officers, volunteer workers, financial supporters, staff members, and others. Many people have given their best to this ecumenical enterprise. This history is their story. A profound appreciation is expressed to all.

The primary authors, named in the Preface, are profoundly thankful to the Rev. Rodney R. Romney, senior pastor of the Seattle First Baptist Church and recent Vice President of the Church Council, for tying the whole volume together in the Epilogue.

Constance Wentzel, retired university and local United Church of Christ administrator, gave indispensable service as editor in the final preparations. At earlier stages, helpful editorial assistance was also given by the Rev. David L. Aasen, retired United Methodist pastor and long-time Council associate; June Whitson, Methodist lay leader and Council volunteer; and Angela Ford, executive assistant to the Council's President-Director, who served on the working editorial committee. Tamara Broadhead, graphic artist, designed the front and back covers. Anne and Merle Dowd have given technical computer assistance in preparing the text for the printer. Enough words of praise and gratitude cannot be found to thank each of them.

For their many courtesies, gratefulness is also expressed to staff members of the University of Washington Libraries, particularly in Manuscripts and Archives, where the Council's historical records are stored, and in Special Collections, where old Council photographs are preserved.

This volume has been financed, in part, by the following: Plymouth Congregational Church (UCC), Seattle, Winifred Weter, Edith Metzler, and others. The authors and the Church Council wish to thank them for their generosity. By means of their help, the net proceeds from book sales will be added to the Council's Endowment Fund.

Finally, close family members of the primary authors deserve recognition and appreciation for the hours lost to them as this book was conceived, drafted, revised, checked, and massaged during innumerable hours at each writer's home and in meetings at the Church Council office.

Preface

In 1994 the Church Council of Greater Seattle observed its seventy-fifth anniversary. The year 1995 marked the twenty-fifth year of operation under the current philosophy and organization of the Council. The year 1996 is the centennial of the birth of the Rev. Gertrude L. Apel (1896-1966), longtime ecumenical leader in Seattle and Washington State.

To celebrate these milestones, it was decided to publish an historical account, a permanent record of the past. It was to be of such a format that many of the faithful would wish to have a copy in order to preserve some memories of their ecumenical experiences. Further, it was to furnish future Church Council members and leaders with secure rootage as they move into new fields of service, witness, and mission in the decades ahead.

So it was that Jessie Kinnear Kenton, Council executive staff member from 1961 to 1982, and sometime Council historian, called together a small group to undertake this task. Initially, there were retired executive heads—the Rev. Lemuel Petersen (1959-1968) and the Rev. William B. Cate (1970-1990). The Rev. Elaine Stanovsky (1990-1995) soon joined the endeavor.

It is only coincidental that the major sections of this volume seem to revolve around the four executive heads of the Council since the

1930s. If it is not readily apparent, it should be stated explicitly that these individuals were products and servants of their different eras. They were not themselves fully responsible for the tone of the Council; rather, they were enablers who facilitated the functioning of the Council to meet the needs and demands of their respective periods.

Through the last three-quarters century, the Church Council of Greater Seattle, in its various forms, has meant many things to many people—individuals who can now be numbered in the tens of thousands, if not hundreds of thousands. On some occasions the Council has been vilified, crushed down, and threatened with extinction. At other times it has been hailed, glorified, and lifted up as being a manifestation of God's will for our times.

Because of her unusually lengthy and significant leadership of ecumenical work in Seattle and the State of Washington (1930 to 1958), this book is dedicated to Dr. Apel. Having been a pioneer woman clergy leader and nationally hailed Council administrator/prophet/ foundation builder, may her memory long live among us.

As the Church Council of Greater Seattle looks toward the third millennium, it moves ahead with great hopes and aspirations. It scans the horizon in hope of a world at peace,

 Where justice may be done to *all* peoples,

 When *everyone* might be gathered together in a greater
  spirit of unity under the ONE God who brought ***all*** into
  existence and yearns for the ultimate good of each and
  every creature,

 "...that they all may be one...."

I

The Founding Decade, 1919-1929

Jessie Kinnear Kenton

THE INTERNATIONAL ecumenical movement was born at the World Missionary Conference in Edinburgh, Scotland, in 1910. However, it had begun earlier in the United States, as expressed through councils of churches. In 1895, the New York Federation of Churches and Christian Workers in New York City was organized. In 1908, the Federal Council of Churches followed.

Any discussion of ecumenical work in Seattle must include mention of nation-wide efforts in cooperative church work: the American Sunday School Union, the Home Missions movement, the Young People's Society of Christian Endeavor, the Young Women's Christian Association, the Young Men's Christian Association, and the Women's Federation.

During the nineteenth and early twentieth centuries, many independent agencies were formed by church people from various traditions to support a variety of good causes and needed reforms. These causes included peace, temperance, Sunday Schools, the abolition of slavery, and women's suffrage. Such agencies laid the foundations for later cooperative work by churches and denominations nationally, as well as in Seattle. In time, the Women's Federation, Home Missions

1

Council, and the Ministerial Association merged with what was then called the Seattle Federation of Churches to become the Council of Churches.

Early Developments

In 1902, a state-wide series of meetings by dedicated laypersons resulted in the formation of the Inland Empire Sunday School Association and the Western Washington Sunday School Association. Both organizations stated as their goals: "to promote the interests and efficiency of the Sunday School." As the two units in many counties of Washington State became the only interdenominational agencies for church school programming, the names were changed to the Inland Empire Council of Christian Education and the Western Washington Council of Religious Education.

Another thread running through the early history of conciliar work was the Home Missions Council, which also began with national work in the Home Missions field. Later, in 1934, the Home Missions Council and local Councils of Churches merged with the state organization which then became the Washington-North Idaho Council of Churches and Christian Education. That name continued for the conciliar work of Seattle/King County and the State of Washington until 1959.

Ministerial Associations

In 1928, an organizational meeting for the interdenominational Seattle Ministerial Association was called by H.F. Burgess with Frank S. Bayley as speaker. Officers elected included: W.P. Roberts, President; Ward McHenry, Vice President; Ed Fuller of the Council of Churches, Secretary; and A.O. Kuhn, Treasurer. Limited to clergy, the informal fellowship continued to operate until 1937. As many as seventy clergy were present at a regular Ministerial Association meeting to discuss the "Kernahan" evangelism visit, and they willingly pledged $3,500 to fund the visit—this, at a time when the Council of Churches was struggling for survival.

The preamble of the suggested constitution for the ministers' group stated: "Recognizing that the co-operative work of the churches is done by the Seattle Council of Churches, this Association is organized solely for the purpose of fellowship among the ministers of Seattle."

An illustration of this policy occurred in May, 1928, when the matter of Vacation Church School Teacher Training was referred from the Ministerial Association to the Educational Committee of the Seattle Federation of Churches. An international exchange of clergy with British Columbia was also referred to the Federation of Churches. It is apparent that the Ministerial Association was a professional group, interested in clergy matters only, while the Federation was expected to organize and lead the service programs of the Seattle churches.

With twenty-two members present at their May, 1937, meeting, the Ministerial Association voted to merge with the Council of Churches. The work of the Council was strengthened and this set the pattern for future ecumenical strategy.

At the same time that the work was strengthened by mergers there were also divisive factors among the churches. One of these divisive factors was the independent nature of the churches. Although this phenomen was not unique to this area, William B. Cate, a national leader familiar with the Pacific Northwest, recognized that by 1932, particularly in Seattle, "ministers...are more or less individualistic."

The membership of the churches of the Northwest was made up primarily of immigrants from Germany, the Scandinavian countries and the British Isles, who brought with them stability and community life as part of the "American Frontier." Dr. Cate, however, portrays the influence of the frontier on American Christianity this way:

> No other factor contributed more to the triumph of a dissenting revivalist form of Protestantism in American life than the frontier. It provided a far-flung social setting congenial to the 'Gospel of the Disinherited.' It provided a frontierized Protestantism. The 'church of the frontier' could be characterized as a sect-type church which was pietistic, moralistic, revivalistic, individualistic, untheological and which drew a sharp line between itself and the world.
>
> *The Nature of the Church.... 1st Pacific NW Faith & Order Conference*

The frontier roots of churches in the Northwest may have accounted for their being "more or less individualistic" in spirit, as Dr. Cate commented. This, in turn, may have been the cause for the later observation by some across the United States that in Seattle, cooperative ministry such as chaplaincy and institutional ministry was twenty-five years behind other parts of the country.

Nonetheless, following the nineteenth century frontier period the Pacific Northwest became a more settled agrarian territory. The frontier sect became a rural church, and as more metropolitan urban areas developed, the rural church became more formal and structured as it became more urbanized. In a variety of ways Christians began to explore and work together.

While churches began working together across denominational lines in a limited way, the "frontier church" and the churches' previous experience did not make the new venture an easy one. An example of denominational and parish needs having priority over ecumenical needs can be seen in the failure of the churches to fund ecumenical work adequately and in the attempts of church leaders to control policy of the ecumenical agency by withholding support. The concept of a "Protestant church for Protestants" also clouded the ecumenical experience, but there was real effort to move together in solving some common problems.

Thus, by 1919, the stage was set for the development of ecumenical work in the Pacific Northwest.

The Seattle Federation of Churches

First steps to organize the Seattle Federation of Churches were begun in 1918 by Roy A. Guild of the Commission of Interchurch Federation, a unit of the Federal Council of Churches in New York, and the Rev. James E. Crowther, pastor of the First Methodist Church of Seattle. In Seattle on June 16, 1919, Ed Fuller of the First Methodist Church, working with the planners for the Seattle Federation of Churches, received a letter from Dr. Guild, reporting that local church federations were being organized in Los Angeles, San Francisco, and in Portland, Oregon.

The first organizational meeting for the new federation was called in July, 1919. Only one person attended. A second meeting was called on July 22, 1919. This time representatives of sixty-two congregations approved a constitution for the Seattle Federation of Churches. Two delegates were allowed each member church with an additional delegate for every 300 members above the first 350. Temporary offices were established in room 306 of the YMCA Building and July 27, 1919 was designated Federation Sunday. E.V. Shayler was elected President and Ernest Tippett was employed as Executive Secretary.

By the time of the first annual meeting of the Federation on

May 5, 1920, twenty churches from fourteen denominations were supporting or had indicated their interest in joining the Federation. Cooperating churches during those years, as stated on a 1922 letterhead, included individual parishes of the following denominations: Baptist, Christian, Congregational, Episcopal, Evengelical, Free Methodist, Friends, Methodist Episcopal, Methodist Protestant, Presbyterian, United Presbyterian, and United Brethren.

In 1923 the Federation officially became the Seattle Council of Churches, although for a time the terms "Federation" and "Council" were used interchangeably. On November 20, 1924, after five years of operation, the Federation/Council adopted a constitution. And so the work began. Though records are incomplete for the period 1924-29, the Federation continued to move forward with officers, program and budget.

Personalities and Staff—Ecumenical work in the Seattle area was shaped by remarkable men and women who felt called to "work together in Christ's Kingdom." Both clergy and lay people who were perceived as valuable leaders in their own churches and the community have given unstintingly of time and leadership to the work of the Federation and of the Council.

At the first Annual Meeting of the Seattle Federation of Churches held at Plymouth Congregational Church, May 5, 1920, according to the Board minutes, the following officers were elected:

H.R. King, President (recognized in later years as the
    Founder of the Seattle Council of Churches)
R.E. Pretlow, First Vice-President
G.T. Hunter, Second Vice-President
Ambrose M. Bailey, Third Vice-President
W.S. Gruger, Recording Secretary
R.H. Michael, Treasurer
F.A. Ernst, Finance Committee Chairman

It is not known which churches they represented.

Among pioneering churchmen were such well-known personalities as Mark A. Matthews, Russell F. Thrapp, Cleveland Kleihauer, U.G. Murphy, James S. Crowther, W.H. Bliss, A.S. Elford, W.R. Sawhill, E.K. Worthington, R.N. Orrill, F.H. Luce, Abraham Vereide, Roy H. Campbell, Bryan Wilson, Charles Mook, Marvin Sansbury, Lucius Baird, and M.E. Bollen.

In 1923, the President of the Seattle Federation was Russell

Thrapp, and the Executive Secretary—the paid staff—was the Rev. H. E. Chatterton. Russell Thrapp was succeeded as President in 1924 by Ambrose Bailey, pastor of First Baptist Church.

Crisis After Crisis—Financial difficulties for the Federation were apparent from the beginning. In July, 1919, at the formation of the Federation, gifts and pledges, along with denominational quotas for support were accepted by the representatives present. Almost immediately, difficulty was encountered in securing operating funds.

The total budget for 1919 was $3,419, of which $1,500 was in borrowed money. In August of that year, Executive Secretary Ernest Tippett was employed as the first paid staff member at a planned salary of $416.66 per month. This was later reduced to $250. A part-time secretary, Hazel Loomis, was employed at $150 per month. It is obvious that these two staff items had already exceeded the modest 1919 budget.

That same month a letter to Dr. Tippett from Dr. Guild of the Commission of Interchurch Federation stated:

> My greatest concern in the organization of the Seattle Federation was that we were doing the work in the summertime. When I found that certain men were for the Federation good and strong, I kept on with the work. I am sure as they settle down to the winter's work everything will swing into line, though as I stated and you re-state in your letter, there will be a good deal of creaking of the machinery. This is the case in every city. I do not think in any meeting the action was more fully discussed and more clearly understood than in the meeting at Plymouth Church when the different denominations fully discussed the amounts, adopted their quotas and appointed their committees.

It was decided to press for financial support from the denominations as well as the congregations. In another letter to Mr. E.K. Worthington of Seattle, Dr. Guild predicted, "Five years from now Seattle will be one of the greatest Federations in the country, as Seattle is coming to be one of the greatest cities."

Finances, however, proved to be an almost insurmountable problem. The Seattle Federation was unable to pay the National Federation for the expenses incurred by Dr. Guild during his organizing visit. The Board of the new Federation decided that they could not pay those expenses from borrowed money but would have to wait until they were able to raise the funds from the giving of the churches.

In writing Dr. Guild on October 14, 1919, Dr. Tippett suggested that:

> ...indeed the machinery is being tested and it is creaking considerably, but I believe it will gradually wear in and run smoothly. During the three weeks I was away no one did any of the things agreed to before I left. Mr. King, Mr. Gruger, Mr. Shank and some other leaders are away east. I am afraid some of the enthusiasm has died out, but I believe it can be rekindled. Our biggest problem just now is money. Nobody seems to feel any responsibility for the amounts I copied from your notebook in Pittsburgh, nothing seems to have been done since the meeting when these amounts were accepted by a few individuals for the denominations they represented. Not a cent has been paid in and we have an empty treasury. Therefore, instead of finding, as I had understood to be the case, that finances had been provided for two years ahead and I would be able to attend exclusively to the activities of the Federation, my first problem is financial. As an illustration, the Episcopalians say the Bishop approved of the $1,000 and that he will apportion it to the churches, but as he is at present in the east, nothing can be done about it.
> I am having to exercise all the Christian patience I can muster.

In May, 1920, Ernest Tippett's annual salary of $2,500 had not been paid since the previous December. Receipts since August, 1919, had amounted to $6,084, but there was a balance of $188.58 in the treasury, with liabilities of $2,474.60. The financial situation of the Seattle Federation did not improve, and in April, a weary Ernest Tippett resigned by telegram, stating:

> My resignation probably will do more than any other thing to save the Federation. Fine determination to continue shown in executive meeting today, but necessary to proceed on a more modest scale and without me. Generous appreciation was expressed but responsibility was never shouldered and now a subtle and powerful influence is working to destroy all cooperative endeavor....This is a heart-breaking job here. I have been used to hard ones but this is pretty nearly putting me under.

In August, 1920, the Rev. H.J. Chatterton, a Presbyterian minister and YMCA Secretary from Everett, Washington, was employed as a part-time Director at a salary of $250 per month. This was in spite of the fact that the Federation President, H.R. King, had favored closing the office and staffing with a voluntary secretary. Part-time secretarial help was arranged on an hourly basis for a total of $687 for the remainder of the year. Helen Bushnell, Marjorie Harrison and Orrill James are mentioned as efficient office help.

The Finance Summary read as follows:

Seattle Church Federation
1919-1923 Financial Summary

	Total Dollars	Number of Churches
1919	$1,918	25
1920	2,475	39
1921	5,085	30
1922	4,365	37
1923	2,858	29

The individual churches were giving from $5 to $1,700 annually, the largest supporter being the First Presbyterian Church with a gift of $1,700. When that support was withdrawn in 1923, the Council's financial condition became critical. In 1924, First Presbyterian Church withdrew from the Council, stating in a letter from S.C. Dalsback, Clerk of the Session, that "the Council is not functioning as an evangelical, evangelistic Council." Following a series of letters between Council leadership and Pastor Mark Matthews, the break was healed temporarily, with assurance from the Council that it would "devote its attention to evangelistic work, live within its means, bring churches into a more spiritual atmosphere, and function as a church organization." With that assurance, First Presbyterian once again began to give financial support to the Council, but at the rate of $50 monthly, instead of the $150 previously given.

The seriousness of this action was illustrated by Roy Guild's statement on March 31, 1933: "Because of opposition on the part of Mark A. Matthews and some others, the Council was nearly wrecked."

The attempt to control Council activities through the withholding of financial support strengthened the belief that the Council's base of support must be so diversified that a single contributor or church could not dominate policy in this way. In the ensuing years, crisis after crisis developed, and it was only through prayer, faith, determination and hard work that the Council was able to struggle along.

By 1928-29, church giving was down to a mere $235 from a high of $5,085. These gifts were all voluntary and no staff was planned. Financial crises threatened even this small operation of the Council. As the economic depression deepened, churches were hard pressed to keep their buildings open. Ecumenical work had low priority in their budgets.

Issues and Concerns—From the outset the Council was ambivalent in its choice of issues to be addressed, and a struggle was always apparent. Such values as community and civic betterment, clean city government, gambling, anti-dancing, anti-prostitution, Sunday blue laws to keep stores closed on Sunday, and Sunday movies reflected a personalized pietistic viewpoint. Those leaders particularly interested in this viewpoint found themselves serving on the Morals Committee, the largest and most active committee of the Federation. The Morals Committee and later the Civic Affairs Committee stated that they were for decency in motion pictures, against race track gambling, for temperance, against juvenile delinquency, for marriage and home and for amending the state constitution to permit school credit for Bible study.

On the other hand, there were those who had a broader world view and a concern for international affairs, justice, peace, and social action issues. The International Goodwill Committee, another active Council committee, had the responsibility for international affairs and matters of conscription, disarmament, amnesty, race relations, and overseas aid. They were also against Federal immigration laws which included a Japanese exclusion section.

From this rocky beginning the Council limped along, but always moving forward. No one wanted to let it die.

II

New Beginnings, New Leadership, 1930-1939

Jessie Kinnear Kenton

In SEPTEMBER, 1930, Dr. Lucius Baird, President, wrote: "The Council of Churches is being resuscitated but there is little hope of our getting on to a vigorous Council program until the churches have been drawn together again by common thinking over local problems that can better be handled through cooperative action than otherwise."

And so the decade begins: Lucius Baird calling for cooperative work and common thinking on local problems, but with finances shaky and direction vague.

The Rev. Gertrude L. Apel

From the beginning there had been no women in decision-making roles at the Seattle Federation of Churches. When Gertrude Apel was employed to begin work as General Secretary of the Washington Council of Religious Education, she had defeated three male competitors, but "all of them might well have been delighted at the outcome," for she found a divided staff, plus organizational debt. One of Miss Apel's advantages was that she had the benefit of having served in the state for ten years in rural, town and urban settings, mostly east of the Cascades. Therefore, she soon was able to gain the confidence of the Council's membership.

Long recognized as a leader who got things done, Gertrude Louise Apel, following her preparation for the ministry in Chicago, had gone to Montana to organize church work in that difficult place. This was two years before her church permitted women to preach. She then held a pastorate of five appointments in central Washington, followed by a six year pastorate in eastern Washington. From there she came to Seattle to serve a northend church.

With hardly a chance to wind up her last job and settle into her new position as General Secretary, she set out immediately for fall regional conventions at Spokane, Walla Walla, Yakima (each a one-day affair), and Seattle (two days), all during the first week of November. During her first year a busy round of other activities followed, including, in part, overseeing twenty county and district conventions, attended by two thousand church school leaders, and thirteen leadership training institutes in Seattle and other major cities, attended by a thousand.

By 1934 the county and district conventions had grown to thirty-six with attendance of forty-four hundred, the leadership training schools to eighty-four with 8,340 participants, and twenty-five other leadership classes. In addition, in Seattle there were 101 vacation church schools with 135 participating churches and nine thousand pupils.

During these same years the Rev. Miss Apel was meeting with the leaders and Boards of the Seattle Council of Churches and King County Council of Christian Education (formerly, King County Sunday School Association, which traced its origins back to the early 20th century). In 1934 they also merged to become the Seattle Council of Churches and Christian Education. In fairly short order, the two Councils had both accepted Miss Apel as General Secretary.

She had the unique ability to bring to a successful conclusion every project that she initiated, and in so doing she imparted to her co-workers a generous portion of her own zeal and enthusiasm. It was said, "It is a joy to face any problem with her, as she drives into the heart of a matter with the keenest insight. A tremendously hard worker herself, she inspires others to spend themselves freely also."

A gifted administrator, she was well-known for her speaking ability and was recognized as a "Master of the Art of Cooperation." She would seek out and wait for a spirit of cooperation to arise in a group and would then use her talent to develop a plan readily received by all. She did not believe that rules and regulations or statements of principles were the solutions, and she was not much interested in passing resolutions. This was at a time when the very young ecumenical movement was caught in what was for the state of Washington a still-deepening period of major economic depression.

In 1934 the Seattle Council of Churches and the King County Council of Christian Education merged. The Washington Council of Christian Education was expanded to become the Washington-North Idaho Council of Churches and Christian Education. In the process Dr. Apel assumed increasing responsibility for the Seattle Council.

She said in November, 1934, "In Seattle all of our departments are headed up by volunteer workers." The Washington-North Idaho Council of Christian Education letterhead she used noted that the organization was a merger of the Western Washington and the Inland Empire Sunday School Councils. It was affiliated with the International Council of Religious Education, headquartered in Chicago. This same letter refers to "terrific pressures... this fall." One can read between the lines the wistful hope that in 1935 or 1945 or perhaps 1955 these pressures might be reduced.

In 1935, the financial picture began to change ever so slightly. On February 7, 1935, the budget for the Seattle Council was adopted at $4,000 with $2,000 coming from individuals and $2,000 coming from churches and denominations. The expense budget of $4,000 was divided as follows: $2,800 as the Seattle Council of Churches share to the State Council budget and $1,200 for the local Council. The $1,200 would be used in the following manner: $800 for rent, stenographic help and postage, and $400 for miscellaneous expenses. No local staff was planned. Evidently Miss Apel's salary was included in the state budget. This recommendation from the Finance Committee to the Board caused quite a discussion. The Executive Committee decided on a two-month delay "when we would determine our official commitment." Apparently there was some concern about the amount of the state budget support but nothing further was reported on the matter.

On January 4, 1935, the two councils adopted a comprehensive statement entitled, "Working Agreements, Policies, and Procedures." These principles continued in operation until the end of 1958.

The essence of the Agreements was that the two bodies would function "more effectively with a joint staff, headquarters and budget." There was a Joint Advisory Administrative Board. Also, the same individuals served both agencies in budget, finance, and personnel. Program was carried out by the joint staff. A significant organization and program were developed with this plan. It gained national recognition in its day.

In 1936, Seattle churches and individuals contributed $2,700 to the state Council with $600 coming from local corporate gifts. Thirty-two churches were listed as members.

State and City Councils Blurred—By 1938, the affairs of the Washington Council and the Seattle Council had become even more blurred, especially in finances. Each organization still maintained separate officers and programs but often they overlapped. The Washington Council finance report showed anticipated income of $9,105 with expenses of $9,078 and a deficit of $2,436. This deficit included back salary for secretaries in the amount of $462 and for the General Secretary, Gertrude Apel, of $875.

Seattle finances showed $4,803 pledged by individuals and $1,139 from the churches for a total of $5,942. Seattle showed a deficit from the previous year of $1,566.

By 1939, the budget for Seattle and the state was $15,000. This included salaries of $6,800 and indebtedness of $1,600. The staff included the General Secretary, Office Secretary, Field Secretary and part-time youth worker. Because there was one program, staff, and budget, no longer was it clear how the staff was operating in and for Seattle, who was paying, and in what amount. The 1942 budget of $25,269 included salaries of $9,969, emergency defense work of $2,000, home missions of $3,200 and youth work of $1,500. Income was expected as follows: $10,000 from individuals, $1,500 from churches in Seattle, $3,400 from across the state, and $5,369 from other sources.

Although the financial situation was critical, the Council of

Churches persevered. At times the finance problems caused the struggling organization to reduce staff and in some instances to close the
offices for a brief period of time.

Increasing Cooperation—The Seattle Council of Churches and
the Council of Christian Education merged in May 1934. The Preamble to the Constitution of the new Seattle Council of Churches and
Christian Education reads:

> Whereas, in the providence of God, the time has come when it
> seems fitting more fully:
> To manifest the essential oneness of the Christian Churches of
> Seattle and King County in Jesus Christ as their divine Lord and
> Savior,
> To bring the churches into united service for Christ and the world,
> To secure the concerted efforts of the churches affecting the
> religious, moral and social welfare of the people,
> To promote the application of the teachings of Christ to all the
> relationships of life,
> Therefore, the delegates of the merger conference of the Council of
> Churches and the Council of Christian Education do thereby
> recommend the following plan to the Christian bodies for their
> approval.

Although the Preamble showing concern and intent was accepted
in May, it was not until October, 1934, that the new constitution and
bylaws of the Council of Churches and Christian Education was
adopted. Twenty-eight churches along with the YMCA and the
YWCA were listed as contributing members. An additional twenty-
two churches, including the Salvation Army, were participating but
not contributing members. The American Bible Society was listed as
participating but not contributing.

In 1936 the Seattle Federation of Women and the Council of
Churches merged. The President of the Seattle Federation of
Women, then called United Church Women, thereafter served as one
of the Vice Presidents of the Council. With the employment of Dr.
Gertrude Apel women had begun to take an active role on the Executive Board and committees of the Council of Churches. Women came
to be valued more highly in ecumenical work, largely due to Apel's
powerful leadership.

With the state and Seattle Councils under one executive and with one staff, work began to blossom in the late 1930s. Staff was hired, and many departments were formed. The United Christian Youth Movement was organized.

In 1936 the Council sponsored a National Teaching Mission attended by five thousand persons at the Civic Auditorium in Seattle. This Mission and the laboratory schools, inaugurated by the Department of Religious Education for Children, indicated the continuing and growing interest in religious education. Five schools of released time were operated under the Department of Religious Education of the Council.

The Council provided service to local churches, both large and small, in whatever areas help was needed and requested, such as Sunday School teacher training, Bible School, and other leadership training. The value of such service cannot be overestimated. It was of excellent quality and for many of the smaller churches it was the only help available. The stated value of service to the local church continued to motivate the Council for many years.

An interesting example of Council influence on community action was evidenced when at a meeting of the Board of Directors on December 6, 1934, the Industrial Relations Committee of the Council was asked to decide the location of the Longshoreman's Union Hall. The committee heard advocates for the two sites and recommended a Pike Street location just below the Pike Street Market. The Union Hall was built upon that recommendation and remained at that site until the late 1970s.

Peace and Justice Issues in Seattle—In 1931 the Commission on International Justice and Goodwill of the Board of Directors of the Seattle Council named three areas of concern:

A. Sino-Japanese Controversy

B. World Disarmament Conference in Geneva, Switzerland

C. American membership in the World Court

The Council was starting to flex its muscles on international affairs when the following message was sent to President Herbert Hoover in 1932:

We urge the government to use its full influence in conjunction with the other powers and preferably with the cooperation of the League of Nations to the end that the conflict between China and

Japan may cease. We urge use of diplomatic and economic sanctions against any government refusing to arbitrate differences.

Board minutes record that 9 foot by 20 foot posters were available with billboard space donated. Twenty posters were already displayed. They read:

CIVILIZATION OR DESTRUCTION WHICH?

The World Faces This Question at
Geneva in 1932
Write the President—Disarmament Conference
Must Not Fail

Churches were asked to band together to supply funds for one or more of the posters ($7.30 per poster) in each community. This was but one of a growing number of Council actions opposing worldwide militarism.

In 1932 the Council's Peace Committee appeared before the School Board to protest high school pupils being recruited for summer military training camps. Thirty-four copies of a second protest were sent to the University of Washington regarding the University's attitude on compulsory military training.

A report from the Council's Committee on National Defense dated October 12, 1933, requested:

1. Substantial reduction in existing armaments.
2. No rearmaments.
3. Abolition of aggressive weapons within a definite period and with immediate elimination of all bombing from the air, of air weapons in general and of poison gas.
4. Limitation of expenditures to prevent rivalries in armament.
5. Effective supervision of existing armament or arms manufacture and trade.

In a letter to President Franklin D. Roosevelt dated December 11, 1933, the Council expressed opposition to the recognition of the USSR. If Russia were recognized, then the Council wanted a condition of that recognition to be protection of ministers in Russia, and religious freedom for propagation of the Christian faith.

Another resolution of the Board put the Council of Churches on record as protesting the persecution of Jews in Germany. This action was released to the newspapers.

A scathing editorial, dated January 22, 1936, in the *Seattle Post Intelligencer* stated: "The Federal Council of Churches in America is a large, radical, pacifist organization. It probably represents 20,000,000 Protestants in America. However, its leadership consists of a small radical group which dictates the policies....of organizations which, while not openly advocating the 'force and violence' principles of the communists, give aid and comfort to the communist movement and party."

The Executive Committee of the Seattle Council responded to the *Post Intelligencer*:

> WHEREAS, the Post Intelligencer, owned by Mr. Randolph Hearst, carried an editorial on January 22, 1936, definitely linking the Federal Council of Churches of Christ in America with communism and;
> WHEREAS, frequent editorials in the Seattle Post Intelligencer imply that churches and church organizations all too frequently are involved in subversive activities and;
> WHEREAS, such charges are deliberate attempts to curtail freedom of speech and freedom of religion and to cause prejudice, misunderstanding and confusion in the minds of church members and non-members...
> BE IT RESOLVED by the Executive Committee of the Seattle Council of Churches that the Council vigorously resists and condemns the editorial policy of the Post Intelligencer urging the adoption of news for its own value and not for propaganda purposes.

In 1937 Claude Eckhart, of Plymouth Congregational Church, was elected President of the Council. On April 5, 1937, the Council supported a nationwide radio peace broadcast with Mrs. Eleanor Roosevelt, Admiral Richard Byrd and Dr. Harry Emerson Fosdick. The Council urged the churches to hear it.

Continuing concern over the Sino-Japanese clash brought a letter directed to the pastors "to consider an embargo of shipment of war goods with letters to be sent to President Roosevelt and to Secretary

Hull." A silk stocking embargo by individuals, but not by churches, was urged.

In September of that year, prayers for the Munich Conference were requested and a telegram was sent to the President concerning the matter.

In 1938 the matter of preventing shipment of scrap iron and munitions to Japan was referred to the Committee on International Justice and Goodwill of the Council with the question: "Can the Council speak for the churches of Seattle?"

John B. Magee of the First Methodist Episcopal Church was elected President of the Seattle-King County Council of Churches in 1935, going from that position to the presidency of the Washington State Council in 1936-37. In 1936, J. Warren Hastings, of the University Christian Church, became President of the Seattle Council, E.A. Fridell of First Baptist Church was First Vice-President, Miss Daisy Jane Trout of the YWCA was Second Vice-President, and Julius Cathcart served as Treasurer. Dr. Gertrude Apel was listed as Secretary of the Seattle Council.

III

The War Years, 1940-1949

Jessie Kinnear Kenton

As THE United States became increasingly involved in the war in Europe, the Council of Churches exhibited serious concern about the Selective Training and Service Act of 1940. A meeting was held to address the particular issue of conscientious objectors. Attorney Arthur Barnett of the Society of Friends and Professor Floyd Schmoe of the University of Washington co-chaired the Committee on Conscientious Objectors. A year later, Professor Floyd Schmoe requested a Conference on Second-Generation Japanese in the Northwest to discuss the problems of this group in relation to the situation in the Far East. The Conference was carried out by another group, and the Council of Churches was invited to attend.

At the Annual Meeting on January 20, 1941, President C.M. Ridenour's message stated: "Too often in times past, it has seemed to be the policy of the individual churches of Seattle to go their own way, but today, the problems are too tremendous for any one congregation or even denomination to think they can face the issues alone. Dictators may say 'divide and conquer' but the slogan of the churches must be 'cooperate or perish.' It is high time for Christians to unite for a more effective action on undergirding the spiritual foundations of our community."

On March 31, 1941, L. Wendell Fifield, Chair of the Civic Affairs Committee of the Council of Churches, presented "The Religious Aspects of Seattle's National Defense Program." D.E. Norcross presented the folder of the National Council for the Prevention of War entitled, "If America Enters the War, What Will I Do?"

A *Seattle Times* news article dated December 2, 1941, stated, "The Rev. Dr. Paul McConkey, Pastor of First Presbyterian Church, spoke at the Seattle Council of Churches meeting saying, 'Next month may give us a Christmas present of a full-sized war, but God grant us that a spirit of hate doesn't get into our churches'."

Five days later the Japanese bombed Pearl Harbor. What had been so dreaded had happened, and the United States went to war with Japan. In short order, the Seattle Council of Churches and Christian Education became fully involved in the war effort. Its help was sought in various war-related activities. For example, in November, 1942, a letter from the National Nursing Council for War Services came, pleading for more nurses. It read: "The Churches can be a mighty force... We request that:

1. Nurses' Day in the Churches be observed.
2. Enlist eligible graduate nurses in Red Cross, the first reserve to Army and Navy Nurse Corps.
3. Recruit student nurses for training.
4. Bring inactive or retired nurses back into the profession (100,000 were estimated).
5. Recruit and train volunteer nurses' aides."

The Army/Navy called 3,000 graduate registered nurses each month, stipulating only that they must be unmarried and under forty years of age.

Church Council Service to the Armed Forces—The Ministry to the Armed Forces Service Center located at the YMCA in Seattle, where as many as 32,000 young GI's found "a home away from home," was a significant ministry of the Council of Churches during the war. Young men found every kind of service there, including housing. Local churches invited the servicemen home for dinner and for many church-sponsored events during their stay in Seattle at Ft. Lawton, the naval base at Pier 91, the Sand Point Naval Air Base, the

Bremerton Navy Yard, and nearby Ft. Lewis. In 1947 it was noted that two hundred women gave 3,191 hours to the Service Men's Center desk at the YMCA. Dr. Apel often officiated at wedding ceremonies for the young servicemen.

The Council sponsored a Hostess House, where service men and their wives could stay for short periods. There also was a Council of Churches Service Center in downtown Seattle where many of the Council's war-related activities were carried out. In one month 9,191 persons used the Service Center for counseling, other "important" interviews and information. It was estimated that between Hostess House, the Service Center and the Ministry to Armed Forces at the YMCA as many as 92,000 young service men were helped.

Relocation of Japanese-Americans

The Council maintained that internment of Americans of Japanese ancestry was an act of racial prejudice. There were three phases of activity resulting from this position. The first was to lobby against evacuation. The second was the organization and promotion of religious, social and educational programs among evacuees, particularly in the assembly centers. The final phase provided assistance to Japanese-Americans returning from internment camps, through the operation of a relocation hostel.

A February, 1944, resolution of the Board of Directors stated, "We recommend that loyal Americans of Japanese ancestry be permitted to return to their homes as soon as the military situation permits; further, we pledge ourselves to do our best to cooperate in their integration back into the community. To ask some Americans of Japanese ancestry to serve in the Armed Forces and confine others of unquestioned loyalty to restricted areas seems wholly inconsistent."

That same spring, the Committee on Race Relations sought the Bar Association's advice on matters of real estate contract discrimination against non-Caucasians.

A letter to Mayor Devin of Seattle and Sheriff Callahan of King County expressed the Council's appreciation for their fair-play attitude in regard to returning Japanese-Americans. Still, the churches' responsibility in the matter of returning American citizens of Japanese ancestry to the Pacific Coast was of continuing concern to the Council. In January, 1945, the Council wrote to the churches stating the need for sponsors. Both the Council's Displaced Persons Program and the United Ministry to Help Returning Japanese-Americans were begun.

Alternative Service for Conscientious Objectors—In 1944, the Council wrote letters regarding the possible parole of conscientious objectors to tax-free hospital service. The parole was to be accomplished through the Council of Churches. The government was slow to respond to this suggestion.

The Atomic Bomb—Harold Jensen, President of the Seattle Council of Churches, wrote in a telegram to President Harry S. Truman on August 9, 1945:

> We take no pride in the development of the atom bomb.

Strong opposition to the bomb was indicative of the peace efforts of the Council.

The Post-War Years

In 1948, in an open letter regarding universal military training, the Council stated that the United States had failed to grant amnesty to 15,805 Selective Service violators. The matter of imprisoned conscientious objectors was referred to the Social Service and Welfare Committee for action. It was noted that only 147 of 4,700 Jehovah's Witnesses had been freed. In the previous 150 years eight amnesty proclamations had been issued; consequently, there was good precedent for another one after World War II. At least fifteen other nations had already granted amnesty at that time. This letter was issued on March 15, 1948, just three years after VJ (Victory in Japan) Day.

Meanwhile, in response to overseas need for relief supplies, American Overseas Aid, of which Church World Service was a member agency, collected and sent 150 carloads of Eastern Washington wheat.

In 1945, the issue of relationship among the local, state, and National Councils of Churches was resolved, at least temporarily. A paper dealing with this stated, "It is clearly recognized that each local Council is autonomous. Our clearly organized local Councils function as the accredited auxiliary units of the State Council. Accredited local Councils usually carry in their constitutions a statement such as 'this council shall function locally as the accredited auxiliary of the Washington State Council of Churches'."

In 1948, plans for a Protestant building to house the two Councils and a number of denominational offices was placed in committee for study by Clinton Ostrander, President of the Seattle Council. After several years, plans for the $300,000 Protestant building faded, and were finally shelved. In 1954 the offices were moved to the Racine Building at Fifth Avenue and Virginia Street in downtown Seattle where they remained until 1970.

An Interracial Clinic to study discrimination was held in 1945. George Haynes, Executive Secretary of the Race Relations Department of the Federal Council of Churches in New York, was the major speaker. A report on Seattle hotels refusing Negroes as guests was given by Mrs. Roy Green of the YWCA. Other issues, such as restrictive housing covenants in Seattle, were discussed. Some lamented that only twenty-eight people were present. Others felt that at least it was a start in the right direction.

In 1949, a Council Board luncheon considered the matter of discrimination in employment, because of color, race, or creed. After lengthy discussion, the Council endorsed legislation to correct discriminatory practices.

IV

Continuing Concerns, 1950-1959

Jessie Kinnear Kenton

A GREAT CHANGE in finances came about between 1950-1962. At first, it appeared that the Working Agreements, adopted in 1935, were operating in the intended fashion. The budget for 1954 for the combined Washington and Seattle Councils was listed as $186,864. This reflected the inauguration of the unit system of giving, whereby individuals were urged to contribute in units ($12 annually per unit). Many contributed such odd amounts as $84, $108, or $144 annually. Such a large budget was difficult to raise even with new creative ideas, but the size of the staff and program seemed to make it necessary. The program across the state and in northern Idaho was well regarded and successful.

The source of financial support for local ecumenical work was long understood to be local churches and interested individuals, with minor support coming from denominational sources. Financing for state ecumenical work had been stated to be "...by appropriation of its just quota by each denominational body. The next best method is to ask for appropriation from the funds of the stronger local churches." According to this view, it was assumed that the state organization could also draw on local parish support.

Conflict continued in the Council because of differing priorities between those concerned with issues of personal piety and morality and those concerned with issues of peace and justice. Ambivalence in setting priorities continued. With limited time, energy and finances, it was difficult to set or change priorities. Many times decisions were based on the strength of leadership in the Council committees.

Membership in the Council—In 1950, the Admissions Committee (Membership) voted to recommend the Reorganized Church of Latter Day Saints for membership in the Council. Nothing developed regarding this decision. However, in 1991, under the Church Council of Greater Seattle, the larger body of the Church of Latter Day Saints was granted Observer status. In1957, membership was refused to the Vedanta Society on the grounds that it was not an evangelical Christian group. Later, in 1984 the Vedanta Society was granted Observer status.

Civic Public Affairs Committee—The Civic Public Affairs Committee of the Council, formerly the Morals Committee, took seriously its constitutional commitment "to secure the concerted effort of the churches...in measures affecting the religious, moral and social welfare of the people." The committee met regularly in the 1950s to discuss varied concerns: gambling, Sunday closing of stores, vice conditions, the Gold Cup races on Sunday, laws and law enforcement, and a host of other public and private morality measures.

On some occasions the Council was representative of the most liberal of the churches' views, such as support of fluoridation of the city's water. At other times the Council represented the most conservative church viewpoint. This is evidenced in its opposition to Sunday dancing at the Eagles Auditorium, the Boeing Sunday Christmas Carnival for Kids and the opening of Longacres Racetrack in Renton.

Racial Equality—Although not organizationally a part of the Council, Christian Friends for Racial Equality (CFRE) began in 1954 with Mrs. Walter Hiltner as President. It was a significant activity, embracing many Council-related members. Other officers of the one hundred member group were: Donald Kruzner, Superintendent of

King County Schools; the Rev. John Gibson, of Plymouth Congregational Church; the Rev. Wayne Griffen, Methodist clergyman; Bertha Pease Hartzell, Methodist educator; and Nora Hatter of Mt. Zion Baptist Church.

Overseas Relief—The postage stamp project to support United Church Overseas Relief was started in 1954, and continued until 1986, through the devoted work and leadership of Andrea Olsen. Her faithfulness and her dedication continued well into her nineties. In her later years, she would come to the Council offices, struggle up the three flights of stairs and disappear into her small secluded stamp room. Surrounded by package upon package of stamps, she would gamely try to keep up with the tide of used postage stamps which came to her from all over the world. At closing time Marge Cheney, the secretary of the Washington Association of Churches would take her home to her small apartment. The stamps were her life. The joy of knowing she was helping to feed the children of the world with the results of the sale of stamps was her reward.

Clothing drives, established in 1954, secured fifteen thousand pounds of clothing and six hundred pairs of shoes for overseas relief during that year. Church World Service trucks would tour West Coast churches collecting clothing and blankets which were processed and sent overseas from northern California.

Continued Growth

Under the unflagging leadership of Gertrude Apel, conciliar work continued to grow in strength and service in Washington and northern Idaho. With the offices of the Council and many of the denominational headquarters located in Seattle, the hub of activities necessarily centered there.

By 1945 a large paid staff was employed with key leadership coming from Council and denominational staff based in Seattle. These key people were sent out across the state and into Idaho to head up leadership and teacher training in the smaller cities and the rural areas. The success of such leadership was clearly felt by the denominations and churches. In 1947, there were as many as twenty-seven paid staff serving in twenty-one different departments. The budget was $70,919 and most staff positions were full-time.

The 1954 roster listed the following:

General Secretary, The Rev. Dr. Gertrude Apel;

Secretary to the General Secretary, Kaoru Ichihara;

Directors of Departments: Public Relations, Eva Bowman; Women's Work, Norma Duncan; Research, Dr. Arthur Frederick; Civic Affairs/Special Projects, Harold Herman; Migrant Work, Mr. and Mrs. Soren Kring; Overseas Relief and Youth Work, Gerald Pelton; Armed Services and Institutional Ministry along with International Justice and Goodwill, Chester Ramsay; Audio Visuals, Ida Terras; Children's Work, Ida Terras; Leadership Education, Duncan and Ramsay (temporary); and Business and Finance, C.W. Thompson.

Office staff included: Office Manager, Ersa Savage; Receptionist, Frances Fullerton; Bookkeeper, Amy Hatsukano; Librarian, Andrea Olsen; Typists and Stenographers, Marjorie MacRae, Rose Yoshizumi, and Dorothy Slick.

Augmenting the paid staff were hundreds of volunteers. A well-organized, active Council became involved in many different areas of cooperative work.

Finances and Support—In spite of the amazing progress that was made, long-standing problems persisted. From the beginning, ecumenical work in Seattle suffered from inconsistent financial support. Several times the Federation and later the Council nearly collapsed from inadequate financial undergirding. Such struggles were experienced in other cities across the nation but they seem to have been exacerbated by the independent "do-it-yourself" spirit in Seattle.

At times, church contributions were reduced or withheld because of a particular program or stance of the Federation. At other times, economic depression or recession made it impossible for the churches to underwrite ecumenical work at the expense of local church operation. At best, ecumenical work did not have high priority in the budget process of the local congregation.

Sanderson Study

By 1957, continuing concern over a high budget, a deficit of over $17,000, and the confusion between the two Councils led to the implementing of a self-study. Council authorities turned to a national expert in state and local ecumenical work, Ross W. Sanderson, to analyze the two Councils, and to make some recommendations. Sanderson made his report in February, 1958. In his conclusion, "An Imaginary Tape Recording," he soliloquized:

> The Council of Churches came to Dr. Sanderson and said, "I'm a schizophrenic personality—ambiguous, ambivalent, inadequately articulated in my inner body. I'm several people in one body, at least two ecclesiastical corporate entities functioning in one corpus. I have two sets of directors, two constitutions, two series of meetings, but only one program, one office, one budget, one staff.
>
> Who am I?...Am I twins accidentally equipped with one brain?...The financial blood that flows out through my arteries goes to the far corners of the state and even into northern Idaho; but the dollar stream flowing in toward my heart appears to come chiefly from Seattle and King County, and there is some evidence of late, that there is 'tired blood' in my veins..."

Earlier in his report Dr. Sanderson had pointed out that although King County represented only twenty-nine percent of the state population and sixteen percent of the state's Protestant membership, the Seattle area was providing seventy-one percent of the financial support for the combined state and city Council budget. His conclusion: "...the 'state' Council is disproportionately financed in Seattle."

The Joint Advisory Administrative Board adopted Dr. Sanderson's recommendations to separate the two bodies, and to make a new start, beginning January 1, 1959. Consequently, after a quarter century of joint operation with distinguished results, Dr. Apel accepted the inevitable, and resigned July 1, 1958, thus ending her many years of service.

Separation of Seattle and State Councils

The separation of the Seattle Council of Churches and the Washington-North Idaho Council of Churches followed. There were some lingering concerns, such as churches not making ecumenical work a high priority, churches trying to control Council policy by withdrawing financial support, and the lack of involvement with the Roman Catholic Church and other Christian denominations.

The path toward cooperative work, which differed from the independent "frontier church" viewpoint of their previous experience had not been easy. However, the ecumenical movement was firmly entrenched by now, and over the span of four decades many churches had learned that, particularly on matters of social action and concern, more could be accomplished by working cooperatively with other churches than by acting alone.

For four decades there had been real progress in moving together to solve common problems. Each success strengthened the resolve to continue to do together those things which can better be done in unison.

V

Four Major Accomplishments, 1959-1969

Lemuel Petersen

TERMINATION of the lengthy and distinguished leadership of the Rev. Gertrude L. Apel in 1958 marked the end of an era in the Council's history.

The years of Council enterprise from 1919 to 1958 were modeled on a philosophy and program orientation that had prevailed nation-wide throughout the first half of the century. It was largely one of serving member congregations/denominations in ways they could not do for themselves. At the same time councils mobilized church inter-ests in community service projects and occasionally gave witness on important social justice issues.

However, during the 1950s various currents had begun to set the stage for new ways of thinking about ecumenical work. In the 1960s these external forces were accelerated. By 1970, when the new Church Council of Greater Seattle sprang forth, a decisive turning point was taken in ecumenical functioning and thinking.

The intervening decade can be seen as transitional. The Council could no longer be what it had been – however, it could not yet be what had to come. In retrospect, it can be recognized that there needed to be a gestation period for a *new* ecumenical entity. Therefore, during this decade the Council continued certain traditional tasks, gradually phasing out some of them, or finding new homes for them elsewhere. Despite tensions, ambiguities, and uncertainties of this in-between mode, the Council was able to accomplish a number of significant achievements, including re-thinking the nature and functions of a metropolitan ecumenical body. In this manner it was preparing the way for what was to be.

During this period the chief executive officer was the Rev. Lemuel Petersen. He served from January 1, 1959, to June 1, 1968. Initially, he held the traditional title of Executive Secretary, but then to emphasize the ministerial/religious role of the Council's executive head, the position was called Executive Minister.

The Setting

In 1959 the City of Seattle was headed by a young mayor, Gordon S. Clinton, who was known as being "squeaky clean." He was strongly identified with Seattle First Methodist Church as well as the Council, for which he had been recording secretary and legal counsel. After serving a second term, Mayor Clinton was succeeded by Dorm Braman, former finance chairman of the City Council, who, despite his conservative outlook, became supportive of the civil rights movement and the "War on Poverty."

The City Council consisted mainly of older men, many of whom had been in office a long time. They were essentially a conservative, business-oriented group. However, there was one Council woman, Myrtle Edwards, who was also a member of the Council of Churches' Executive Committee. The first Council member from a minority group was Wing Luke (1962-1965), followed in 1967 by Sam Smith, a well known state legislator. Both were active church members.

The Seattle Public Schools were strong, not yet involved in problems of school integration, ethnic diversity, multi-lingual students, drugs, crime, and similar problems that came later.

King County government was still run by a three-member Board of Commissioners, and was concerned only with unincorporated areas—some of which were rather extensive and well populated, such as Burien and Shoreline. METRO (the Municipality of Metropolitan Seattle) had only recently been authorized to take care of water and sewer treatment.

At the state level Albert Rosselini, Democrat, was governor. He was a Roman Catholic lay person, liberal in political and social orientation. He could be counted on to support such issues as minority rights and improvements in the correctional and welfare systems. He appointed people of national stature to head these departments. Daniel Evans, a young Republican member of the State Legislature, became governor in 1965, and served for twelve years. He was liberal in civil rights, welfare, corrections, and other causes in which the Council was interested. As had been the case for years, control of the State Legislature moved back and forth between the two political parties with mixed results.

In terms of church life, among the mainstream denominations there was a strong evangelical following. In many congregations there were unresolved tensions between liberal and conservative elements. Unlike eastern cities, however, Seattle was fortunate to have large, thriving congregations downtown and on nearby First Hill. When added to the major parishes ministering in the University District, these institutions were a solid feature of Seattle's moral and religious landscape. Many of the senior ministers were well known and respected in the city. Also there was a strong constituency of the Seattle Evangelical Ministers' Association, a small number of whom were ecumenically minded, but most holding the Council in suspicion. Lastly, there were a few small, mostly ineffective fundamentalist churches.

Although the population of Seattle was near the half million mark, the general culture of the area was still basically that of a conservative small town. Having greatly expanded during World War II, the city had not yet in the 1950s caught up with the wider world. It took the 1962 Seattle World's Fair—more properly, Century 21 Exposition—to change this mix.

Just as 1959-1969 was a transitional decade for the Council, providing the springboard for a much larger and more potent ecumenical body to come, so the body politic of the Seattle area was gathering momentum for a grand burst of population, physical development, and cultural expansion which was to follow in the 1970s and 1980s.

Major Achievements

At the risk of slighting program activities which will be mentioned in the next chapter, at least four major accomplishments during the 1960s can be identified, and are therefore treated here in more detail.

Providing a Christian Presence at the Seattle World's Fair

Mobilizing Council-related churches as well as some congregations from non-Council denominations—plus a variety of Christian agencies—to sponsor a Christian Pavilion and Children's Center at the 1962 Seattle World's Fair was a major task of the early 1960s.

Sited adjacent to the U.S. Science Pavilion (which became the successful Pacific Science Center), the handsome Christian Pavilion was visited by 900,000 visitors during the six-month fair. Its architect was Robert Durham of Durham, Andersen, and Freed, well known for having designed many churches in the area.

Major Attractions—Significant features of the Christian Pavilion included:

A religiously oriented child-care program, in which 13,155 children were enrolled. It was the only place on or anywhere near the Fair grounds where parents could leave young children. It provided two-hour periods of the best in quality Christian education activities. It was directed by Margaret Woods, professor of creative education at Seattle Pacific College. In preparation, a planning committee, headed by Melba Petersen, Christian educator, curriculum writer, and public school teacher, had defined the basic operating principles, prepared a curriculum handbook, and recruited and trained an elite corps of volunteer teachers.

A small theater, with a brief "sound-and-light" film, written and produced on commission by Sacred Design Associates of Minneapolis. It had a theological message on the themes of creation, redemption, and consummation. Because it was presented in an abstract format, there were many complaints that the film could not be understood. On the other hand, some persons thought highly of this innovative effort to reach individuals who were not traditional Christians.

Two major pieces of art work produced specially for the occasion: a stained glass window on the front facade, which when lit at night was a great attraction, and a large wood chip mosaic panel of Christ and the children inside the entrance, leading the way to the Children's Center. The window had been contributed by the Stained Glass Association of America, which, after the Fair, sold it to a Roman Catholic Church in St. Paul, Minnesota. The wood chip panel was purchased by the Gethsemane Lutheran Church of Seattle for its main entrance, where it can still be seen.

A meditation chapel, where volunteer chaplains were on duty, and services conducted by the various sponsoring member bodies on Sunday evenings.

A gift shop, where souvenirs, such as Bibles, New Testaments, note paper, bookmarks, and postcards, all with Christian Pavilion photos or logos, could be purchased.

In addition, throughout the Fair special programs were staged by member denominations and agencies. Each week a different member body would take responsibility for activities which might be held on and/or off the Fair grounds. An example was "Ecumenical Week" from May 21-28, sponsored by the Seattle and Washington-Northern Idaho Councils of Churches.

Another special event was a Billy Graham rally, held on Sunday afternoon, July 8, in the adjacent high school stadium under the co-sponsorship of the Council, Seattle Association of Evangelicals, and the Century 21 Exposition.

A Complicated Project Realized—Beginning in April, 1959, a series of exploratory meetings with exposition officials and denominational representatives was held. By June, 1960, it had been decided to incorporate a separate agency to be known as Christian Witness in Century 21, Inc. (hereafter referred to as CWC21). Throughout the life of the project the president was Luvern V. Rieke, Lutheran lay leader and professor of law, University of Washington.

CWC21 membership included twenty-one denominational judicatories of the Pacific Northwest and fifteen other agencies, such as the Seattle and Washington-Northern Idaho Councils of Churches, American Bible Society, and other national, regional, and local church-related bodies. Some of these did not usually participate in Council activities.

Continuing the role already assumed by default, the Executive Minister served as secretary for the new corporate body and its Board of Directors. By March, 1961, it was apparent that he needed to give more time to this project. Therefore, the Council Board released him to work as executive vice president for CWC21, at first part time and then full time.

For all of 1961 and 1962 the overwhelming concern was to raise sufficient funds to finance the project. Proceeding on faith, by the end of February, 1962, construction of the Pavilion was ahead of schedule. However, the original budget of $175,000 had grown to $268,000.

The precarious nature of the project can be seen in that by the end of April, 1962, it was forecast that CWC21 would have obligations of $102,190—an amount approximately $12,000 more than the total raised in a whole year. But somehow through the grace of God and hard work the Pavilion opened on time and operated the entire 182 days of the Fair.

Even so, a month after the close of the Fair, CWC21 was still trying to complete financial obligations. With all sources of potential revenue exhausted, the balance owed was $26,000.

By year's end, it was acknowledged that "The Greater Seattle Council of Churches through its staff and office [had] made an unusual contribution. ... In terms of financial assistance alone, the Council wrote off its books the sum of $11,448 due from Christian Witness for staff salaries, thus making one of the larger cash contributions of member bodies to this ecumenical project."

In retrospect, it can be affirmed that CWC21 took a heavy toll. For about a year and a half the Council was diverted from its main tasks. It was several months before the Council was back on track. And yet, when all is said and done, the Christian Pavilion, the children's center, and the whole panoply of programs were eminently worthwhile.

Giving Leadership Support to the Civil Rights Movement

As the Council's earlier story unfolded, it was seen to be frequently in the forefront of human rights efforts. This emphasis continued throughout the 1960s, being a dominant priority, especially for the five-year period of 1963-1968.

Right from the start, open housing was a concern. In January, 1959, the Council's Executive Committee, acting on business carried over from the previous year, approved in principle the 1959 proposed amendment to the State Civil Rights Law (House Bill 70) with special emphasis on cemetery and housing clauses. In that initial month the Council newsletter also circulated "The Good Neighbor Pledge." However, because of the many problems which attended the separation of the state and Seattle Councils and because of the urgent need to rebuild finances and program, the Council was precluded for a time from pressing ahead with activities in this field.

Fortunately, into the breach came Seattle United Church Women (UCW), who offered stickers to members and churches, which said, "I am a customer who would welcome being served by those whose race, creed, or color may be different than my own." Many Council constituents participated in this low-level campaign. They applied stickers to personal bill payments and correspondence with business firms. From time to time other well-intentioned efforts on a modest scale were recorded.

A Primary Focus on Race—At first, tentatively (in the years of President John F. Kennedy) and then urgently (during the administration of President Lyndon B. Johnson) the Council kept pace with the moral challenges of the human rights crisis of the nation. With the completion of the World's Fair project there was once again energy for the Council to give major attention to civil rights.

Following up a national assembly held in early 1963, a Seattle Conference on Religion and Race (Catholic, Protestant, and Jewish) was held at Seattle University on June 5, 1963. With approximately four hundred in attendance, it was a high point of church-community involvement. The co-chairpersons were the Rev. Samuel B. McKinney, Mount Zion Baptist Church; Fr. Jack Lynch, St. James (Catholic) Cathedral; and Rabbi Jacob Singer, associate rabbi, Temple de Hirsch, Seattle. The Council's Executive Minister was staff coordinator. This conference provided the springboard for an intense period of interfaith, community-wide action to follow.

The first concrete action was a Freedom March, held Saturday, June 15, 1963. Several hundred participants, with a good mixture of Afro-Americans and whites, started from Mount Zion Baptist Church and walked downtown. Many had never taken part in such an event. It was a bright sunny day. The mood was one of exhilaration. The march was orderly and proceeded without incident. The police provided an escort. On arriving downtown, relieved that no provocations had occurred, people dispersed in a semi-holiday mood.

With these events, race became a major agenda item. In addition to reports of the interfaith conference, the June 12 Board meeting also heard an account of recent developments between department store heads and civil rights leaders regarding more adequate employment of minorities. On the following Monday, June 17, the Bon Marché was to be targeted for a demonstration protest. However, when negotiations with the Bon proved fruitful, the march was directed toward City Hall, at which time Mayor Clinton came out to speak to the assembled group.

After the Board heard reports on these actions, the discussion then turned to the role of the Council. The recording secretary summarized, as follows:

> It was pointed out that though no one can speak for the Council, that in matters where justice and injustice are involved, Council leaders as representatives should speak as their best judgment indicates. Also in any declarations as far as great Christian traditions are concerned, they should speak not only with respect, grace, and love, but justice. It was the feeling that the Council of Churches would have to carry much of the burden for whatever is done from a religious view of race relations; that the role of the Council is to assert as much of our Christian principles as possible in the framework of our communal structure.

The Board then voted to accept the reports of President Everett J. Jensen and the Executive Minister, and expressed continued confidence in their good judgment.

At a later meeting the Council's Vice President for Business and Finance, B. Franklin Miller, observed "that though...the Council [would] probably lose some financial support because of what has been done in the racial matter...the good gained by standing up for what we feel is right will far outweigh any loss."

During the next few years, as a result of this kind of support, Council officers and the Executive Minister were often in the front ranks of street marches, demonstrations, and behind-the-scenes negotiations. They were called upon innumerable times to speak, not only to churches but also to schools, civic and business groups, and other gatherings. They often called together key political, business, educational, and community leaders to meet with clergy of the major Afro-American churches and leaders of the civil rights groups in order to hear their concerns and to discuss how they could be met.

Probably the most tangible role of the Executive Minister was that of being one of only two white persons (the other being Fr. Lynch, representing the Most Rev. Thomas A. Connolly, Catholic Archbishop of Seattle) to serve on the Central Area Committee on Civil Rights. This ad hoc group was composed of leaders from the major Afro-American churches and such civil rights groups as the Seattle Urban League, NAACP, and CORE. All educational activities, social action demonstrations, and other events which required joint participation of various groups were coordinated through this committee. For five years the committee met weekly on Saturday mornings to plan, participate in, review, and evaluate the many joint and separate action projects of the cooperating groups.

The Busy Summer of 1963—Additional events of this feverish summer dealt with the problems of discrimination in jobs, education, and housing. On the job front there were conversations with officials of the Seattle Chamber of Commerce and the King County Labor Council.

Council representatives attended and spoke at a meeting of the Seattle Public School Board about its protracted search for a policy on desegregation of Central Area schools. There was also a meeting with the County Commissioners.

At the same time the officers of the Seattle-King County Real Estate Board declined to meet. However, knowledgeable persons noted that some real estate firms were willing to do business with persons/families of color, and that a Fair Housing Listing Service had been organized in various parts of the city.

As a climax to an exuberant summer, the next Freedom March occurred on August 28, followed by a service of prayer at Seattle First Methodist Church.

CURE: Mobilizing for Open Housing—The next major activity followed in late 1963 and early 1964, originating with the Denominational Executives Advisory Committee. In addition to the seven major Protestant denominations represented in that group, many other churches and agencies cooperated in this three-month special effort called Churches United for Racial Equality (CURE). Its purpose was to obtain a favorable vote on March 10, 1964, for a proposed open housing ordinance in Seattle (as well as Tacoma).

The Council provided office space and use of telephone and facilities while the denominations contributed special funds and staff.

Most notable was the Rev. Paul Beeman of the Methodist Church
Conference Council. Close working relations were maintained with
the Seattle Citizens' Committee for Open Housing, which also had
temporary offices at the Council.

Among the many actions was distribution of 80,000 church bul-
letin inserts, entitled "Love Thy Neighbor," for use on Race Relations
Sunday, February 8. On March 7 demonstration marches started from
various parts of the city and came together at the proposed site of
Westlake Mall.

Unfortunately the housing ordinance was defeated, but for many
years this well-coordinated effort was remembered with favor by denominational and church leaders.

Other Highlights of the Mid-1960s—In June, 1964, the Executive Minister participated in a Saturday night Freedom Patrol, a demonstration protesting a recent case of alleged police brutality. With
the Rev. John Hurst Adams, pastor of First AME Church and chairperson of the Central Area Committee on Civil Rights, he spent the
evening walking throughout the Pioneer Square area, looking for
possible evidence of deviant police behavior.

In March, 1965, as a result of a trip to Washington, D.C., and
Selma, Alabama, in behalf of pending voters rights legislation before
the Congress, the Executive Minister was able on his return to promote widely through the mass media as well as in talks to churches
and community groups the need for legislation.

Working for School Desegregation—A boycott of the Seattle
Public Schools, staged March 31-April 1, 1966, was without a doubt
the most controversial civil rights action. The purpose was to call
attention to the inadequate progress being made on school desegregation. Without specifically endorsing the boycott, the Board authorized Council President McKinney and the Executive Minister to sign
and send a message to the churches. They laid out the segregated
conditions of the Seattle Public Schools, the inadequacy of school
district efforts to that date, the frustrations of civil rights leaders in
gaining the serious attention of school leadership, and urged all
friends, members, and parents to encourage the School Board to adopt
a plan for school integration. To many, such a message was tantamount
to endorsement of the boycott.

To ensure a creative follow up, during the next month the Council engaged in two activities. The first was a luncheon meeting on April 13, 1966, of the Council Cabinet with members of the Seattle School Board, the superintendent, and administrative personnel.

The second effort, held April 28, was a day-long Clergy Workshop on Racial Imbalance in the Schools, for which the Council took the lead. Co-sponsors were the Catholic Archdiocese and Jewish rabbis of Seattle. The purposes were to consider constructive steps for effective communication between the minorities and the white majority, to broaden the public's understanding of the de facto segregation problem in the school system, to review what had been done and could still be undertaken to correct imbalance, and to suggest ways the clergy and churches could assist in meeting this problem.

In the long view the school boycott probably served to expedite later efforts to integrate the Seattle schools. Of immediate significance, the action brought Council officials and school authorities into closer communication for the rest of the decade than they had been before.

Despite Setbacks, Perseverance—Although the Council paid a price, suffering reverses among some of its constituency and in parts of the business community, it did not flinch. It continued its leadership support role. At the 1966 fall meeting of the House of Delegates (as the church delegate assembly was called during these years), a committee was approved to "investigate, analyze, and offer recommendations regarding the alleged social discrimination in private social clubs, fraternal groups, and churches."

In 1967 the Council assumed sponsorship of a program known as Interracial Dialogue. It conducted a day-long "Open Forum on Black Power," following the Seattle visit of Stokely Carmichael. Transfer of Caucasian students into Garfield High School as part of the program to secure racial balance in public schools was supported. Renewing previous efforts, Council staff also initiated two conferences with Seattle business leaders regarding minority employment problems and opportunities.

In January, 1968, the Council Board authorized a "Message to the Churches" on housing, in which, among other suggestions, it called for "support of a meaningful open housing ordinance with adequate enforcement measures and not subject this time to referendum...."

Sadly, it wasn't until May, after the assassination of the Rev. Martin Luther King, Jr., that the Seattle City Council enacted such legislation. That same year a Department of Christian Education task force on reverse racial transfer in the schools continued the Council's work to enlist exchanges in both elementary and secondary schools. In addition, a youth task force sought to mobilize students and parents who were interested in helping with school integration by providing information by phone.

In 1969, despite the Council's absorption in the process of redesign, and although operating without an Executive Minister, the Board and/or Cabinet continued to take action on several important civil rights issues. For instance, President Elliott N. Couden was authorized to sign a letter from leaders in Seattle to state representatives and national leaders, telling of an impasse with labor union officials over the need to admit minorities into unions. Even as the old Council was winding down, several similar actions were taken.

Strengthening the Bonds of Christian Unity

Full Catholic participation in the local ecumenical movement was also one of the outstanding accomplishments of this era. Nurturing relationships with the Archdiocese of Seattle helped make possible this happy outcome.

Of course, much happened in other circles that warmed the local ecumenical climate. Not the least was the healing pontificate of the late Pope John XXIII and the historic Vatican Council II. Also, in Protestant and Eastern Orthodox circles there developed widespread interest in faith and order and in Christian unity in general.

Faith and Order Concerns—Already in 1959, local interest in faith and order studies was evident. "Faith and Order" is a term which originated in international ecumenical circles to refer to conferences and projects whose purpose is to study and understand the roots, history, current developments, and continuing problems in the movement toward greater unity among the Christian churches and denominations. Following the adoption of a new provisional constitution in January, 1961, a Division on (*sic*) Christian Unity was established. Its purpose was to facilitate such studies as well as general ecumenical education and action.

A major aspect of local interest was preparations for and follow up to three regional conferences, sponsored by the state and metropolitan councils of churches in Washington and Oregon. The first Pacific Northwest Conference on Faith and Order, under the chairmanship of the Council's future President-Director, the Rev. William B. Cate, then executive head of the Portland (Oregon) Council of Churches, was held October 16-19, 1961, at Menucha, near Portland. The second regional conference, chaired by the Rev. Walfred Erickson, Seattle area Baptist pastor and educator, was held in October, 1965, at Buck Creek, a Presbyterian campground near Mount Rainier. This time Catholics were significantly involved. In May, 1969, the third such conference was held at the University of British Columbia, Vancouver, B.C.

In the Council's long-standing tradition of monthly forum-type membership luncheon meetings, the emphasis in the fall of 1961 was "Focus on the Church Ecumenical." The regional faith and order conference at Menucha as well as the forthcoming Third Assembly of the World Council of Churches to be held in New Delhi, India, were featured.

Between regional conferences the Council maintained an active local Faith and Order Committee, which involved key Protestant, Catholic, and Orthodox clergy in fairly frequent theological discussions.

Continuing the Catholic-Protestant Narrative—Undoubtedly, the budding relationship between Catholics and Protestants locally was nourished initially, beginning in 1961, by the interreligious KOMO-TV dialogue program called "Challenge." It featured Father William Treacy, of the Catholic Chancery; Rabbi Raphael Levine, noted long-time spiritual leader of Temple de Hirsch; and the Rev. Martin Goslin, Plymouth Congregational Church (and his successors from other churches). Immensely popular, the program nurtured a public acceptance of closer fellowship among divergent traditions. The time had come for official collaboration.

In January, 1963, the Council's newly re-organized Faith and Order committee invited the Archdiocese to name a representative to the committee. At the same time a close relationship was established with key faculty members of St. Thomas Catholic Seminary in Kenmore, especially with Father Peter Chirico, S.S. This liaison had several important ramifications. In the late spring of 1963 the Executive Minister met with the St. Thomas faculty. He was the first Protestant clergyman to do so. In subsequent years he returned several times to confer with interested faculty and for two years with graduating seniors.

Gatherings for Christian Unity Prayers—In 1965, 1966, and 1967 the crowning event in January each year was a Public Gathering of Prayer for Christian Unity. Scheduled on the first Sunday of the Week of Prayer for Christian Unity, the services were held the first two years in the Seattle Center Arena and the third year in the Seattle Center Opera House. Each year the major attraction was intended to be a noted Protestant and/or Catholic personality, who was invited to speak. But the most compelling feature turned out to be the intense response of several thousand persons who, until then divided by deep historic chasms, just wanted to come together. A spirit of reconciliation crackled in the air. The most joy seemed to be expressed by the Catholic nuns, who were still quite set apart, continuing to wear their black, flowing habits.

In connection with these great public events, informal dinners were held on the prior evening for the various bishops, other executive heads of cooperating denominations, and distinguished guest speakers. These occasions were opportunities to meet as equals around a plain table for a common meal. There were no agenda, no speeches, and most importantly, no protocol.

Laity Involvement—In 1965, following the lead of the Department of Christian Education, the Council co-sponsored with the Confraternity of Christian Doctrine (Catholic) and the Jewish community an Interfaith Convocation on Religious Education. A prominent Episcopal educator, the Rev. Randolph Crump Miller of Yale University Divinity School, was the featured speaker. The event was attended by some four hundred individuals. An elaborate curriculum display with associated teaching materials of all three major groups was a popular attraction.

Beginning in late 1965 and early 1966, the Council collaborated with the Confraternity of Christian Doctrine to establish a wide network of "Living Room Dialogue" groups, consisting of lay members from Catholic and Protestant parishes. The Seattle area was chosen to be the West Coast pilot for this national program. Greater Seattle was divided into twenty-two districts. Twelve to fifteen lay persons (no clergy) were brought together in homes for a seven-month discussion series. They had well-prepared material on ecumenical relations for reading and study. These groups continued for a second year, using as the study guide *The Wholeness of the Church*, the report of the second Pacific Northwest Conference on Faith and Order.

Catholic Membership in the Council—In organizational terms the culmination of these ecumenical efforts came at the Council's fall meeting of the House of Delegates at the Seattle Center on Sunday afternoon October 16, 1966, when six Roman Catholic parishes were received into Council membership. Included were St. James Cathedral, St. Patrick's, St. Luke's, St. Bernadette's, and Our Lady of Fatima, all of Seattle; plus Our Holy Family of Kirkland. The Executive Minister pointed out that although eighteen other local councils of churches had already received Catholic members, Seattle was the largest metropolitan city yet to do so. At the same meeting, five Protestant churches renewed their Council membership; there were also five additional congregations which made first-time applications.

As an expression of his personal interest in the new relationship, Archbishop Connolly invited the Council's Board of Directors to be his luncheon guests at its January, 1967, Board meeting, and to visit the Chancery in a personally conducted tour.

At first, Catholic membership seemed artificial and not well understood. Yet there was no turning back. The relationship was to bear much fruit in the years ahead. At the 1968 Annual Meeting a seventh Catholic parish, Blessed Sacrament Church, was received into membership. At the same meeting the first Catholic to become a Council officer was elected Vice President—Father John (Jack) Mitchell. The Most Rev. Thomas Gill, Auxiliary Bishop, Archdiocese of Seattle, and pastor of St. James Cathedral installed the new officers.

Other Manifestations of Growing Unity—In 1967 there were other exciting activities in interchurch and interfaith relations. The Department of Christian Education was asked to consult on curriculum selection for a suburban church (Normandy Park United Church of Christ) and an inner city, mixed race Catholic parish (Immaculate Conception). Together, they held a joint vacation church school. In 1968 several other schools of like nature were held, and given counsel in curriculum and programming.

Further, because the great Public Gatherings of Prayer for Christian Unity no longer seemed to be the best expenditure of time and energy, it was decided in 1968 to set up twenty-eight areas of neighboring congregations. There was to be a variety of functions, including dialogue, panel discussions, and fellowship over a meal. At the suggestion of Archbishop Connolly the Council instituted pulpit exchanges between Catholic and Protestant churches. In 1969, such events took place in twenty-five neighborhoods.

Working Toward a New Council Entity

Of equal significance during this era was "redesign" of the Council. The process was no less than a decade-long, in-depth, corporate soul-searching review of the philosophical/theological basis for local ecumenical work, the nature of any such organization, how it should be structured, and how its program should be developed and administered.

Although the culmination of this story came late in the 1960s, the whole period was spent in preparation. In fact, its antecedents may well be traced to the 1958 Ross Sanderson survey report, mentioned earlier. Dr. Sanderson raised serious questions that were not then really understood nor considered.

Early Soundings—The next voice was that of the Rev. Donald Salmon, the new chair of the Council's Program Commission. In his first report to the Executive Committee (January, 1959), he cited "Some Hard Facts to Face," starting off with the declaration that "We are in a Rebuilding Period *(sic)*. In some instances we are at a low ebb..." That process began formally on February 16, 1959, when the Executive Committee authorized a group to revise the Council's twenty-one-year-old constitution. With many twists and turns the process of rebuilding was not fully accomplished until 1969/1970.

A frequent refrain of these years first appeared in May, 1959. The Executive Committee minutes reported that it was hoped "to make the Council of Churches truly responsive to the will of the churches, and the churches fully responsible for the Council in all its programs and policies." In his October, 1959, "State of the Council of Churches" report to a monthly membership meeting the new Executive Minister raised the question, "What is a Council of Churches?" The point of view then put forth was, in part, as follows:

...[The Council] is the churches in association to minister to the larger parish – the dynamic metropolitan community that lies beyond their congregations and neighborhoods.... It helps fill the gaps between local churches and their denominations, for by their nature they cannot minister to the total community. Sometimes the Council's function is *to stimulate* the churches to perform this broader ministry each in their own way; sometimes its function is *to coordinate* various programs of the churches, as they desire; sometimes its function is *to administer unified programs* of the churches in this wider outreach... (emphasis above as in original).

Foreshadowing the eventual redesign, the Council's Annual Report for 1959 stated "that the Council is now being defined and interpreted in terms of the churches' total mission to all people and society, thus seeking to make the Council relevant to each congregation in its outreach to the whole Seattle metropolitan community."

Envisioning "Radical Change"—Having had no revision of its constitution since 1938, the new Council leadership immediately concluded that "a complete new instrument" was needed. But the task was to be more than merely writing a new constitution and by-laws. It involved a process that was called "constitutional reform." The object was to secure widespread discussion, debate, and involvement in order hopefully "to discover what the churches really want this Council to be and to do."

Therefore, the next step was to authorize a Committee on Constitutional Reform. The new plan would become effective "when at least five local denominational bodies and at least 50 local churches [had] approved it...." Because the complete participatory process which had been envisioned could not be carried out due to other demands, in early 1961 a provisional constitution was adopted. After extensive discussions among the constituency it was hoped in time that the committee "would be able to present a permanent Constitution to the churches and local denominational bodies for ratification."

A New Start on Rebuilding—Because of the hiatus caused by the CWC21 project, for almost two years nothing happened to carry forward "constitutional reform." So the next approach to redefining the Council's role and program was undertaken with a two-day Council Life Conference on February 15-16, 1963, with the theme "The Ecumenical Calling in a Metropolitan Community." The conference involved new officers, Board members, denominational executives and representatives, and program committee chair persons. In a series of sessions they considered (1) What the Council is; (2) What the Council is doing; and (3) What the Council ought to be doing.

Minutes of subsequent Board meetings record considerable effort to digest the insights from the conference. There were also discussions about how to involve the House of Delegates and church constituency in meaningful followup. However, further attempts to capitalize on these recent gains were eclipsed by other factors, especially intense involvement in civil rights, which soon gained center stage.

A Return to More Traditional Forms—Although unique and provocative, the provisional constitution of 1961 did not "catch on." In fact, due to continuing confusion about terminology and structure, a revised constitution along more traditional lines was adopted February 13, 1966. It became the governing document for the rest of the decade.

And yet, the ink was hardly dry on this document before church delegates were again raising questions about the "appropriate role of the Council." Therefore, at the 1966 fall meeting of the House of Delegates it was reported that the Board of Directors had approved a recommendation that "The Council undertake a thorough study of the Council of Churches in relation to the churches and to the community."

Launching Revision and Reform—The time had come to get the redesign process actually underway. To do so, the Executive Minister set forth a vision and challenge for a *new* Council in a paper, "Toward New Dimensions in Ministry." On November 15, 1967, the Board voted to approve "in principle the Working Paper...with the declaration that the Council is in process of becoming a *new* Council of Churches as a goal for the celebration of its 50th anniversary in 1969."

To implement this declaration, the Board authorized a Special Task Force on Redesign. A steering committee was recruited. The first chairperson was Dr. Adams, local civil rights leader and future bishop in his denomination. The steering committee represented many points of view and a wide range of experience.

When Dr. Adams left for another pastorate elsewhere, the chairperson became the Rev. David G. Colwell, new senior minister of Plymouth Congregational Church (U.C.C.), who had been active ecumenically on the national scene and locally in previous pastorates.

After a year of deliberations, the Task Force reported at length to the 1969 Annual Meeting. It noted that the group was "moving into a new phase," including "broadening the Task Force to make possible the kinds of coordinated planning demanded by any significant change in structure and function of the Seattle Council...." Some of the affirmations were:

> Noting the need for a biblical basis for redesign, "The theological truth about the church of Jesus Christ is that it has an essential unity...that must be readily visible...."

> Questioning the continued viability of a traditional local council of churches, "the long term future of the Seattle Council is in question...in terms of its usefulness as an instrument for the Lord Jesus Christ."

> The problems before the task force must be faced not only by the Council, but also by the denominations, the state council, quasi-independent church-supported groups as well as Ecumenical Metropolitan Ministry and alliances of neighborhood congregations. All must be brought into "the task of working out what God requires of the church for mission to the world in this generation and place...."

The report went on to say:

> Widespread consultations were being held "to determine the possibilities of serious dialogue...concerning major and coordinated changes in structure.... The goal...could be...a look at the whole task of the church..., an examination...of all existing church structures..., an attempt to prepare valid goals for the church...in Seattle..., and finally, ...such deaths and new births in the various church structures as will be required to achieve the goals thus delineated.

At last, on April 21, 1969, the redesign drafting group was ready to make a definitive report. It met with Board members and "Agreed: to accept and approve the direction in which the Task Force...[was] moving as presented in its paper...entitled 'A Proposed Interim Structure' and to encourage a continuation of present Task Force efforts." The next step was to report on May 4 to the House of Delegates.

Finally, on May 28, 1969, having incorporated last-minute feedback, David Colwell presented the finished product to the Board. After minor changes, the Board voted to approve the proposal and to "proceed with suitable implementive procedures."

The final report opened with a one-page, blank verse type of exposition, called "Theological Rationale." Some of the wording was included in the constitution of the new Church Council.

The Task Force then reported that certain denominational leaders were initiating wider conversations to see if there was a possible basis for a new level of unity not only in Greater Seattle but also extending beyond into the state and the Pacific Northwest. As a result, an "interim" structure that would "radically change" the existing Council was recommended.

> The new Council "would function primarily in the areas of: (A) Research—Determination of priorities for urban strategy and the determination of goals for the Church; (B) Training—The preparation of laymen, clergy, and executives for Ministry and Mission in the urban scene; (C) Implementation—The setting into motion the forces which will cause the Research to be translated into program and the Training to be translated into Mission; (D) Proclamation—The bringing to bear of Christian insight and testimony on the immediate and long-range problems which face the metropolis; (E) Innovation—Keyed to (C) above but specifically pointed toward the encouragement and development of new forms of Church life." *(Emphasis and style throughout as in the original text.)*

The proposed interim structure was to be composed of :

1. An Assembly (principally clergy and lay delegates from denominational bodies and local congregations as well as other bodies).

2. A Board of Directors (the "place" for strategic thinking and planning for the Church's mission in metropolitan Seattle).

3. An Executive Council (later changed to Executive Committee) to handle the more or less routine tasks of administration and to set the agenda for the Board).

4. A President-Director, who would combine the functions of both the volunteer elected President and the employed Executive, thus avoiding the confusion which had sometimes prevailed about these roles. (The President-Director would be assisted by a small staff.)

5. A Church Services Agency, "as a relatively autonomous agency"

with three functions: coordination of church-related agencies that need/desire a "central meeting place and clearing house;" service, such as printing, mailing, purchasing, et cetera; and chaplaincy (coordination of various institutional chaplaincy programs).

Rather than build an imposing structure for implementation of program, the Church Council would attempt to use already existing entities, or if necessary, set them up independently of the Council. Task forces would not be used to carry out program functions, but would be "short-term and carefully limited instruments to do specific jobs, primarily in the areas of Research and Training...."

The result was that on December 31, 1969, the *old* Council passed into history, and on January 1, 1970, the *new* Council broke forth upon the Seattle horizon, perhaps like a new-born infant still weak from its prolonged period of gestation, but also greeted with great enthusiasm and hope for the future.

A Quartet of Challenges

During the 1960s, the Council acted as a bridge between older forms of ecumenical ministry and new structures and opportunities. It faced these four major challenges—none of which would probably ever again be repeated—and met them successfully:

It provided a Christian presence in a handsome pavilion at the heart of the 1962 Seattle World's Fair;

It gave support and leadership to the Afro-American churches and community in their quest for greater opportunity and the exercise of human rights;

It fostered historically significant dialogue and official relationships among Protestants, Catholics, Orthodox and other Christians;

It served as agent for institutional change, bringing an old-style Council, well suited to the needs of previous generations, into a dynamic new form with a broader but well focused mission.

At the same time, the Council faithfully pursued its traditional tasks, often reshaping them to respond to the impact of future events.

VI

A Decade
of Transition,
1959-1969

Lemuel Petersen

Pursuing traditional forms of ecumenical ministry during a decade of continual change required ongoing review and new initiatives.

First, some traditional projects were phased out or entrusted to other bodies. Some carry-over programs were kept going only at a maintenance level while others were expanded. Because the decade of the 1960s was a yeasty period both in the ecumenical and general environment, some experiments were tried yet did not survive. Other new ideas were seriously worked on, but didn't get off the drawing boards. Some activities involved the Council in nurturing good ideas that did not come under the Council's umbrella. And as always, there was considerable cooperation with world, national, and state ecumenical agencies as well as assistance to public bodies and their concerns.

Following is a panoply of Council activities not included in the previous chapter. The year 1959 serves as a bench mark. Hints of decline or demise but also of survival and even new life are sketched, including what was still on the Council's agenda in 1969.

Who is to say what activities were really most important—which ones touched the largest number of people? Although the ones which follow may not seem to some observers as significant as the major ones described in Chapter V, individuals who benefited from those which follow might well rank them higher in their scale of appreciation of the Council's significance.

Phasing Out Certain Traditional Programs

In the mode of transition, several time-honored Council activities were carried on for a time, and then for one reason or another were terminated. Some of these involved major public events. Others were for the benefit of the Council's constituency. Two were in the realm of public affairs, inherited from times when personal piety and public conformity were highly valued.

Occasions of Public Worship—For many years the Council had arranged and taken responsibility for Holy Week and Good Friday services in downtown Seattle and the Easter Sunrise Services at Volunteer Park and Washelli Cemetery. In earlier years hundreds, even thousands had attended the latter on Easter morning at dawn. However, by the late 1950s public interest had declined. In 1960 it was decided that these events should be sponsored by neighborhood churches and/or ministerial groups.

Having had a history of notable Council-sponsored performances of Handel's *Messiah* in the old Civic Auditorium, the Council instituted in its place a late November interchurch choir festival held on a Sunday afternoon in one of the leading churches. On November 22, 1959, the second annual Thanksgiving Hymn Festival was held. For a time, similar events took place each fall, the one in 1964 being the last one of record.

Monthly Membership Meetings—Luncheon meetings for church members and others, held at Seattle First Methodist Church on the first Monday (later, Tuesday) of the month, were a major carryover from the past. Maintained for a time, they eventually were altered and then discontinued. For many years the monthly meetings of Seattle United Church Women were held also at the same place and on the same day at 10 AM. The women joined the male contingent for luncheon and a program.

In 1959 a sample of luncheon program subjects and speakers included:

> *March*—Topic, "Worship in an Ecumenical Setting" with the Rev. Joseph Sittler, Lutheran theologian and professor, University of Chicago Federated Theological Faculty.
>
> *October*—Topic, "The State of the Council of Churches," by the Executive Minister.
>
> *November*—Topic, "A New Bet on Unity," with the Rt. Rev. Stephen Bayne, Episcopal Bishop, Diocese of Olympia, on his departure for London to become Executive Officer to the Archbishop of Canterbury.

One 1960 meeting was keyed to the presidential election when John F. Kennedy broke the barrier to a Roman Catholic being elected to the highest office in the land. It featured a debate: "Resolved: That a Protestant Can Vote for a Roman Catholic for President," with two affirmative and two negative speakers.

By October, 1962, in hopes of making it possible for more lay persons to attend, the Council decided to move from monthly luncheon meetings to two dinner meetings per year, in addition to the annual meeting in January. (Note here the origins of fall, winter, and spring meetings of the House of Delegates, later the Assembly.)

Issues in the Public Realm—Among concerns in public affairs, inherited from the past but which lost out during the 1960s because of changing mores, was the campaign "to achieve a non-commercial observance of Sunday." For a number of years an interfaith group, including a Council representative, had been cooperating with business and labor interests to discourage neighborhood stores from operating on Sundays.

By early 1962 it was conceded that because of the ineffectiveness and weakness of the old state law, there was need for new Sunday closing legislation which could be enforced. As late as 1966, a Board resolution on the subject was sent to members of the House of Delegates. From then on, however, this issue no longer appeared in the Council records. There seemed then no way to stop the commercialization of Sunday.

Another public affairs concern was the official city tolerance of certain forms of illegal gambling. In late 1961 the Board of Directors approved two resolutions to Century 21 Exposition officials, the Seattle mayor, and the governor, opposing a proposed gambling ship to be anchored in Elliott Bay and possible Fairground gambling activities—neither of which, in fact, did occur.

In February, 1962, the Board of Directors adopted a "Statement on the Tolerance Policy for Gambling." City officials were urged "to bring the city ordinances into conformity with the state laws." Later in 1962, because of law enforcement problems Mayor Clinton instructed the Seattle Police Department, beginning January 1, 1963, to begin making arrests for illegal, but tolerated public gambling. When the City Council amended its ordinances to conform to the mayor's action, the Board voted commendation for the five Council members who had taken the initiative on this matter. Thereafter, gambling seems to have faded from active concern in the Council.

Maintaining Various Carryover Programs

Being in a transitional mode from 1959-1969, the Council maintained other traditional projects. Because they met important needs, they couldn't be dropped precipitously. Nothing much was done to nurture them; yet they consumed considerable time and energy. Among such activities were ministry to armed services personnel, concern with legislative issues at state and local levels, and information and referral service to the larger community.

Ministry to Armed Forces Personnel—Continuing an inheritance from World War II and the Korean conflict, this activity included weekly breakfasts (called "Java Hour") at the Seattle Armed Services YMCA. Between 25-75 young men participated. (At that time, apparently no service women were in the population group being served.) Transportation was then given to local churches for Sunday morning services. Volunteers from Seattle United Church Women hosted afternoon coffee hours from 4 to 5 PM Saturdays and Sundays as well as buffet luncheons on Easter, Thanksgiving, and Christmas. A Council of Churches Information Desk was maintained. In a typical year (1961) more than 110 women from 28 churches volunteered for this duty. Sunday afternoon sightseeing tours were made available. E.W. Bostrom and Christine Meade were the YMCA liai-

son. The Council had a part-time staff member for weekend counseling. In 1960 a recently retired staff member from the Armed Services Branch, Roy Fleming, was retained as a part-time director, which
function he continued for the rest of the decade.

Legislative Concerns—In the realm of public affairs the Council had an honorable tradition. During the 1959 state legislative session "the former Civic Affairs Committee met several times and proposed actions re a number of matters."

On February 8, 1961, a special meeting of the Executive Committee was held to consider proposed bills before the state legislature.
However, before specific legislation could be considered, the discussion turned "to the making of pronouncements by the Executive
Committee in the name of the churches." Opinions took two opposing directions: (1) efforts should be made to ensure that the Council's
voice and action were more representative of church members' opinion, and (2) the Executive Committee should provide social action
leadership even if it is not always approved by all of the constituency.
Another meeting later in the month (February 24) of denomination-
ally designated representatives provided another forum with similarly
divided opinions.

Two years later (February 4, 1963) the Council Board sponsored
a breakfast for King County legislators in Olympia in order to provide Seattle area participants in the state council Legislative Conference an opportunity to meet their representatives.

Also in early 1963 at the local level the Executive Minister convened a luncheon meeting of two Council Board members involved
in social action plus the president of the Seattle Association of
Evangelicals, the president of the Lutheran Council, and a Greek
Orthodox clergy representative with two new City Council members,
namely Wing Luke and A.L. Kramer. They discussed mutual interests of "gambling, minority housing legislation, urban renewal, and
motion picture classification."

Information and Referral Service—Right from the start, the
Council played a time-consuming, but significant role as an information clearinghouse for the community. The implication was drawn
that "the Council [was] a 'nerve center' in the community." In October, 1959, a tabulation of telephone calls was made for the month as
follows:

	Incoming Calls	Outgoing Calls
Petersen	297	180
Ricker	252	194
Reception	574	79
Other staff	22	33
	1,145	486

In the Annual Report for 1962 it was noted that "thousands of individuals [called] for information about ministers [and churches] here and elsewhere in the nation, and a variety of data about religious and denominational questions. Many queries [were] of a personal nature, persons seeking help with problems of alcoholism, employment, marriage, and family." In addition, "The Council office also serve[d] as a clearinghouse between the churches and many community, business, educational, welfare, and civic institutions."

Even in the last year of the old Council, there was recognition of this service in a program on Radio Station KXA on May 4, 1969, one in a series called "God of the Present." A fifteen-minute program, the format was a dramatic sketch with twenty-eight typical questions and requests that had come to the Council office.

Expanding Other Carryover Programs

Despite the distractions described elsewhere, the Council found energy to meet certain basic needs and also to advance beyond where it found itself in 1959. Among these concerns were several in cooperative Christian education training. Another was the field of pastoral care/chaplaincy services in various public and private institutions of care and correction.

Training Needs of Church Educators—In 1959 the Seattle Council had major Christian education training programs, carrying on one of its more historic functions. That spring fifty-eight leaders attended a Vacation Church School Workshop and two hundred teachers enrolled in a Vacation Church Institute. That fall three Leadership Education Schools engaged 702 workers, and were held in Seattle's north end and southwest as well as on the eastside. More adult education courses were provided. For the first time observation opportunities on three Sundays during October were offered in forty churches with seventy-four persons participating. The Directors of Christian Education Fellowship met monthly for fellowship and in-service training, and continued to do so throughout the decade.

In the fall of 1960 there was some expansion with four six-week Leadership Training Schools, with the addition of a unit in south King County. A total of 118 churches participated. In 1961 nursery laboratory sessions for three-year-olds were held on four Sundays in Bellevue, Kent-Auburn, southwest and north Seattle. In 1963 these were given a new name, Schools of Christian Service. In the last year under the old Council the spring event was reduced to a weekend affair. With the approaching changeover to the new Church Council, nothing was scheduled for the fall.

Other Christian Education Activities—As early as 1959 there was talk about a program for mentally retarded children in coopera-tion with a southside congregation. By 1960 enough churches were showing concern that a survey was made. In 1961 a committee was activated. Various types of experiences during the decade were re-ported. For instance, in 1962 Friday evening sessions at the CWC21 Children's Center were scheduled to provide creative arts for the handicapped. In 1965 a demonstration class was held to aid teachers of such children.

Inherited from the past was a Youth Work Advisory Committee. Adult advisers worked with the Seattle United Christian Youth Coun-cil. For some years an interdenominational rally was held during National Youth Week on the last Sunday of January or the first Sun-day of February. In 1961 the Seattle youth council worked with other groups around the state on plans and programs for teenage partici-pation in CWC21. By 1966 neighborhood churches were encouraged to conduct Youth Week seminars, conferences or institutes. There-after, this traditional type of ecumenical activity faded from the Council's "radar screen."

Pastoral Care in Various Institutions—Pastoral ministry in various institutions of care, correction, and detention was a major concern throughout the whole decade. It was often a priority for ex-pansion whenever funds would permit.

Still operating on a voluntary basis in 1959 (as it was for a large part of the decade), the Council staff arranged for regular services with clergy and/or lay leadership from various churches in city and county jails, Alcoholic Rehabilitation Farm, Salvation Army Men's Social Center, Goodwill Industries, and the Masonic Home at Zenith. In 1960 it was reported that 290 such worship services had been conducted. In 1961 there were 161 ministers and lay persons involved.

In 1962 with the Rev. Neal Kuyper of the Presbyterian Counseling Service as chairman, the Institutional Ministry Committee developed three sections: (1) Hospitals, which met with administrators who had expressed desire for a chaplaincy, and in turn surveyed ministers as to their willingness to be volunteer chaplains and trained for such work; (2) Nursing Homes, including preparing a list of those now being served by churches as well as their needs; and (3) Correctional Institutions, chiefly the King County Youth Center.

Although institutional ministry was to be a priority emphasis in the 1963 budget, the Council had to wait until August 15, 1964, for sufficient funds to move ahead. It then employed a part-time Coordinating Chaplain in the person of the Rev. James Vance, Evangelical United Brethren pastor, who served until 1967.

The next step was the first-time, Council-sponsored chaplaincy class at Swedish Hospital, coordinated by the new Presbyterian-supported chaplain, the Rev. Richard Johnson. It was held in January-February, 1965, and since then has been an annual event.

Work also was carried on with University Hospital and University district ministers to provide on-call chaplains. There was also cooperation with local ministerial associations in similar programs at Burien and Overlake hospitals. Council staff also coordinated training for lay volunteers in nursing homes, with classes on home visitation through the winter and fall Schools of Christian Service.

On another front that year, Chaplain Vance recruited Protestant, Catholic, and Jewish volunteer clergymen to go with State Highway Patrol officers when they had to notify families in King County of the death of next-of-kin. He also gave attention to counseling and education in the field of alcoholism.

In 1968 the Department of Christian Life and Mission secured the part-time employment of the Rev. George McCleave, retired Presbyterian clergyman, as Coordinating Chaplain. Thus, the Council was able once more to offer professional staff and/or volunteer chaplains in most King County hospitals as well as to develop better relationships with their administrators.

Nurturing New Programs Not Under the Council

Through the years the role of the Council to counsel, "hold hands," "open doors," and otherwise assist new projects has been well known. In a major way, support of the civil rights cause was of this nature. But this nurturing role was also to be seen in other ways.

In April, 1959, a series of meetings with the Executive Minister began at the initiative of Seattle United Church Women and the American Indian Women's Service League. Representatives of some twenty churches and civic groups were soon brought together to assist in the establishment of an "Indian Hospitality Center" in downtown Seattle. It was a service center for urbanized Native Americans of Seattle so that they could help themselves.

In 1969 there came a call from certain Seattle Central Area mothers, principally Bobbie Campbell, asking for help to start a drop-in center/club for 12 to 15-year-old girls "on the streets." Council staff (namely, Jessie Kinnear and Betty Phillips) were encouraged to continue meeting with the group. Hopefully the Council could be a catalyst in getting the project started. Their efforts led to the organization of the Central Area Girls Club, Inc., still in operation today.

Also, during 1969 these same staff members participated in community meetings to help establish a day care center organization for the Puget Sound Area. It was thought that such a body would be helpful to the churches as they were beginning to set standards for their own day care centers as well as offer guidance in learning how to secure government funds.

These are but a few of many "outside" organizations/causes which called on the Council with some frequency for counsel and active assistance. In response, Council personnel represented the churches in helping to give birth to numerous programs and agencies where the work of Christ could be carried on under "secular" auspices.

Cooperating in World, National, and State Programs

Inevitably, a local council, although not legally and structurally a part of the World and National Councils of Churches, is caught up in certain projects that require immediate and widespread response. Notable during this decade were the collection of good used clothing, migrant ministry, and "the stamp project."

Collection of Clothing—Contributing garments no longer in use for overseas relief was in 1959 still a significant ongoing activity. That year a typhoon in Japan was cited as the type of disaster to which church people could respond through Church World Service.

During the first six months of 1961 with new volunteer leadership in the person of Veda Graves, wife of a Presbyterian pastor and herself a "promotional wizard," 600,000 pounds (or 300 tons) of good, used clothing were collected and shipped from Pier 91 by the U.S. Navy in a project known as "Operation Handclasp." Destinations were Japan, Formosa (later known as Taiwan), Korea, Hong Kong, Philippines, Alaska, and Haiti. A total of 203 Council-related churches participated. There were 175 volunteers from fifty churches involved in work parties. Beyond Seattle, seventeen communities participated, some as far away as Port Townsend.

Throughout these years, this kind of activity was largely a continuing volunteer project of Church Women United, interested churches, and other groups with minimal, but active Council staff support.

Ministry to Farm Workers and Families—Although the problems of agricultural workers were basically a national and state responsibility, Seattle also became involved. In 1962 there were twenty-four migrant camps in King County with 2,200 workers. Despite preoccupation with the World's Fair, the Council inaugurated a summertime ministry to such workers and their families. A seminary couple was employed for six weeks to work with volunteers in three communities (Fall City and on Bainbridge and Vashon Islands) in a program of Christian nurture, health education, recreation, and fellowship. In 1967 and 1968 attention turned to a Migrant Resettlement Project to help these people, with the aid of cooperating churches, to "settle out" in the Seattle area.

The "Stamp Project"—By 1959 the project to collect U.S. commemorative stamps, largely supplied by women's groups, was in its sixth year. At first, it was a modest effort, nurtured with tender, loving care by Andrea Olsen. When sold to stamp dealers, the resulting cash would be sent to Church World Service in order to purchase government surplus food for overseas relief.

Although technically a project of the state Council, Seattle promotional support was a significant factor in the dazzling success of this long-term effort. The first important breakthrough came in 1960. Ed Mitchell, religion editor of the *Seattle Post-Intelligencer,* spotted a Seattle Council newsletter which featured the project. He picked up the story, elaborated on it, and illustrated it with a large photograph. The account in turn was retold by the Associated Press and sent across the country. In no time, Miss Olsen was receiving hundreds, later thousands, of commemorative stamps from all over the nation.

Whereas it had taken five years to collect enough stamps to bring in $6,000, in the year of 1961 alone, because of this national publicity, approximately $9,200 was realized (which in turn released $350,000 worth of surplus food). The project continued for another 25 years (until 1986), averaging receipts of approximately $10,000 a year for most of that time.

Assisting Public Bodies in Their Tasks

In its first seventy-five years of existence, the Council was called on to work with various governmental offices. In the 1960s these included liaison with and support of the Seattle Public Schools and the University of Washington.

Seattle Public Schools—Already in 1959, conversations were taking place between Council personnel and public education officials about the "problem of having to excuse too many children too often for religious activities." In 1960, another step in this collaboration was a course in one of the fall Leadership Training Schools on "Religion and Public Education," taught by the Executive Minister. He invited the Seattle School Superintendent, Ernest Campbell, to be a resource leader. In no time, consultations were being held between education officials and Protestant, Roman Catholic, and Jewish leaders about the problems and pressures of religious observances in the schools.

As a followup, in 1961 an interfaith committee was more formally organized to meet with the Seattle School Superintendent and his associates to collaborate on these problems of policy and administration. Among the projects which followed were a set of guidelines for principals and the first of several annual teachers' workshops on this topic. For some time, meetings of the interfaith committee continued to be held.

Also in 1961 in what now seems a somewhat quaint move, Superintendent Campbell "directed the school personnel to keep Wednesday nights free for church activities in the school calendar." The Council Board in turn voted to send Mr. Campbell a letter to commend him on his cooperation and to express appreciation for the teachers' workshop.

Whenever Seattle Public School levies were on the ballot, the Council gave formal endorsement. For example, in 1967 following the rapprochement between district and Council officials after the recent boycott, a letter with fact sheet summary and a strong endorsing statement was mailed to clergy, press, and others. In subsequent years there were occasional special meetings (as there had not been before the school boycott) in which Council officials were invited to meet with the superintendent and/or School Board members on the annual budget and levy problems. In early 1969 the superintendent attended a monthly Council Board meeting for this purpose.

University of Washington—In the 1960s and earlier, there had been a void in the scholarly study of religion at state-supported institutions of higher education—due largely to the severe restrictions of the Washington State Constitution, which historically had been narrowly interpreted. In addition, there were occasional rumblings from the then small band of fundamentalist clergy in objection to an academic approach to the study of the Bible and religion.

In1966 the Council staff was asked to help the University of Washington fend off a fundamentalist court challenge to its English Department course on "The Bible as Literature." This action came before the University could offer comparative religion and various other courses in religious studies. At the request of the University's legal counsel, the Executive Minister helped with background research relating to biblical and church/state issues. During the two-week Superior Court trial, he was invited to sit at the side of the University's attorney for consultation. The plaintiffs lost. They then appealed to higher courts, but eventually the University was upheld.

As a result of the Executive Minister's assistance, he was one of three clergymen invited by President Charles Odegaard to a special conference at Packwood to discuss ways and means to broaden the university curriculum in order to include other academic courses on various religious subjects. The other two clergy were Dr. Adams, cited above for civil rights and Council redesign leadership, and Rabbi Norman Hirsch, of Temple Beth Am.

Experimenting with Other New Programs

In this decade of flux and experimentation, it is not surprising that the Council sought to develop certain new initiatives. Regardless of merit, not all were destined to survive. Prominent among them was a promising Lay School of Theology and a vigorous Protestant Committee on (Boy) Scouting.

Lay School of Theology—From 1961 to 1964 the Council offered high level adult Christian education at an upper college or seminary level in the form of a Lay School of Theology. Faculty was drawn from Seattle Pacific University, University of Puget Sound, and Pacific Lutheran University along with local clergy who were academically qualified.

A planning committee designed a three-year curriculum. Each course was to meet for two hours each evening, once a week for ten weeks. The fee was to be $25 for each course, a not so insignificant amount in those days, but hopefully sufficient to make the school self-supporting.

The most popular courses were contemporary Christian theology, Old Testament, New Testament, and Christian ethics. The Rev. Walfred Erickson, pastor of Clyde Hill Baptist Church, Bellevue, was dean, and each evening during the break offered a brief stimulating lecture to all students.

Because the decline in enrollment had become increasingly a financial problem, in April, 1964, the Board voted to discharge the Advisory Committee of the Lay School. They expressed particular thanks to Dr. Erickson, dean, and to Mrs. Virginia Erickson, the registrar, whose volunteer assistance to the Public Gatherings of Prayer for Christian Unity in the mid-1960s was also to be significant.

Protestant Committee on Scouting—Another short-lived project was a committee formed "to stress the Christian purposes of scouting." For a time it met a need, but before the end of the decade it had languished. On January 15, 1961, a consultation of church institutional representatives and troop leaders of church-sponsored Boy Scout units was held with more than one hundred in attendance. One of the major tasks of the committee was to interview and approve candidates for the God and Country Award. During the summers of 1961 and 1962 the committee provided a full-time chaplain, a seminary student, for the newly opened Camp Omache in the Cascades.

Considering Various Program Ideas

Inevitably, there were to be certain concerns that were studied but in spite of their merit did not bear fruit, sometimes for lack of financial support. These included "the youth problem," social welfare, and a miscellany of others.

Youth Problems—Among the several concerns of the decade that were deliberated upon at length were behavioral patterns in the teen-age population. Although the Council had no specific action projects nor staff to deal with them, such problems could not be ignored. Various special institutes and workshops were held. For instance, in 1967 the Council staff participated in the King County Sex Education Steering Committee, which included representatives of public and private school systems as well as important community leaders. Members of the Department of Christian Education reviewed the text of a proposed booklet on drugs for the Seattle-King County Youth Commission.

Social Welfare—For some time, it had been thought that the Council should have a department which would relate the churches to social welfare agencies and ministers to social workers more effectively. It was noted that most metropolitan councils of churches had staff personnel for such services. For several years references are to be found in Board minutes to various discussions of the concept.

During 1964-1965, when funds permitted, a part-time Program Associate for the Division of Social Ministries, the Rev. Herbert Lazenby, Episcopal priest, social worker, and community organizer, was retained for more than a year. Dr. Lazenby provided counseling, referral, and community relations as well as keeping speaking engagements and performing the staff work for the division. During his tenure a Conference on Churches and the War Against Poverty was held (April 5, 1965). When he moved on, lack of sufficient funds prevented the Council from replacing him, let alone expanding his functions.

Other Frustrations—If space permitted, a complete historical account would acknowledge other deficiencies in this decade of transition. Among the more significant ones would be:

Disappointment in being unable to bring the Friends of
Youth, Inc. under the umbrella of the Council (as its
founders had sought).

Failure to respond to early multi-denominational overtures
for an ecumenical counseling service.

Hindrances in establishing a role for the old Council in
urban/metropolitan ministry (though in the near future
such a function was to be a prime focus for the redesigned
Council).

Complications in providing significant witness and action on
issues of peace and international relations.

In many other metropolitan councils such program activities were
integral parts of their structure. Despite investment of great energy
and time in pursuing these possible options in Seattle, this Council
was not to be so favored at this particular time.

Annual Meetings and Administration

Annual meetings of the Council, always held in January during
this time, were the locus of formal legislative authority. "Cut and
dried" as these occasions seemed to be, they nonetheless were important for the following reasons:

An Annual Report—often, a "state of the Council" message
with a succinct review of the past, analysis of the present,
and a generalized look ahead. (A review of these reports
would provide an historical overview of the Council.)

The succession of authority (with election and installation of
officers).

The assurance of financial responsibility and budgetary
integrity (with the numbers for the year past, always
audited by an outside certified accountant to ensure cred-
ibility, and approval of expectations for the year ahead).

Earlier Annual Meetings—For a number of years, the more formal business sessions were accompanied by a meal (at first, a sit-down
dinner; later, a buffet luncheon) and interesting program features. In
1959 when the new Executive Minister was installed, the main speaker
was the Rev. Jerald C. Brauer, noted historian of American Christianity and Dean of the University of Chicago Federated Theological

Faculty. During the next three years the annual meetings followed a similar format.

Then, summoning dormant energies, the 1963 annual meeting took the form of a Council Convocation held at the elegant new Seattle Opera House. After "the faithful" had gathered in a side room to conduct the necessary business, the big event took place on the main stage. About two thousand persons attended. The major attraction was Charles C. Parlin, Methodist lay leader and one of six co-presidents of the World Council of Churches, as the main speaker. The Rev. Roswell P. Barnes, Executive Secretary of the New York Office of the World Council, installed the newly elected Council officers. After having survived a latent period when the Council's regular work had been overshadowed by CWC21, the Council felt a surge of renewal and courage from this Convocation.

Later Sessions—In addition to an annual meeting in 1964, the House of Delegates began holding spring and fall sessions. Each was to have a special speaker on the general theme of the day in addition to "focus" groups which played an important part in Council decision-making.

In 1969, the Council observed its 50th anniversary with three traditional meetings, plus a special gathering of the House of Delegates.

First was its annual meeting on February 2. The featured speaker was the Rev. William A. Visser 't Hooft, first general secretary of the World Council of Churches. Three other notable international guests were on the program.

Observance of its half century jubilee (looking back) and redesign of the Council (looking ahead) were the highlights of the Sunday afternoon meeting on May 4.

In preparation for a final vote to implement redesign, the House of Delegates met on Sunday evening, October 5, to hear and discuss recommendations for the new Church Council.

To make way for the dissolution of the old Council and to usher in the new, the House of Delegates held its final meeting on November 16. The main business was adoption of a new constitution, approval of the report of the Nominating Committee, and action on the 1970 proposed budget. A concluding worship celebration followed.

Financial Concerns

As noted before, difficult financial problems attended the beginnings of the new era of the Council. Many different approaches were suggested both to budget reduction and control and to stabilizing and adding to the financial resources from member churches, denominations, individuals, business firms, and other sources. Despite some short periods of relatively stable financial operations, however, the decade ended without a solution to the fundamental problems of securing adequate financial support.

At the start, the newly separated Council inherited tensions and negative attitudes attendant on the recent breakup of the state and Seattle councils, leaving certain long-time supporters alienated. Due to the historical situation, in which the churches and individuals of Seattle and King County had been major sources of funds for operations of the combined state-Seattle councils, it was expected (in fact, it was a condition of dissolution) that the Seattle Council would assume a significant share of underwriting the newly independent state body. In addition, the terms of the division required the Seattle Council to assume two-thirds of the staff of the former organizational set-up and of the combined assets as well as the obligations.

Seattle was seen as being economically strong, and was thought to be more than able to carry this load. Such, however, proved not to be the case. In three years (1959-1961) the Council expended $49,166 on non-local, non-current obligations ($19,972 to the state Council and $29,194 to contracted obligations). When in 1962 the unpaid CWC21 obligations were added to these earlier "non-productive" expenditures ("non-productive" in terms of fulfilling the program mandates laid upon the Seattle Council), it can be recognized that for at least four years the Council had been required to run a race in a highly competitive environment, carrying an extra heavy weight.

Having gotten off to a somewhat shaky start with a budget built on unknown and unrealistic assumptions, by February 1959 it was found that a $10,000 deficit for the year was a distinct possibility. Consequently, in those early months many attempts were made to make up this difference.

Coming up short, the Executive Committee in May authorized a budget of $73,307 with reductions of $5,500. As a result, three long-term staff members had to be terminated as of September 1, 1959, thus cutting the inherited staff nearly in half.

Happily, by the end of the third year it could be proclaimed that the Council was staying within its income. At the 1962 annual meeting the Council treasurer stated that "Current assets exceed[ed] liabilities and except for current bills the Council [was] virtually debt free..." made possible by "careful watching of expenditures...and by curtailment of the Council's program in line with receipts."

Looking Toward Program Expansion—Toward the end of 1962 an expansionistic view began to develop among the lay finance volunteers. A consensus seemed to develop that the Council officials were "being pikers" in what was being expected from the churches. It was said that in asking for a relatively small amount, the importance of the Council and its program was being downgraded. Therefore, the Council should raise its sights in both program expansion and in what should be the churches' share. Consequently, both the 1963 and 1964 budgets contained priority projects if funds should become available.

With this point of view prevailing, by the time the 1966 budget was adopted, it had a deficit of $8,497. However, on a positive note, there were two gains. For the first time there were to be unemployment compensation for the clerical staff and a retirement plan for full-time lay executive staff.

Difficult Years Return—Financially, the middle 1960s proved to be rough ones. In mid-summer, 1965, the budget had to be trimmed and funds borrowed for operations, the most in this decade. By 1967 the precarious financial situation of the Council was increasingly evident. In order to balance the budget (for the first time in two years) the position of Administrative Secretary was terminated. Even so, the annual deficit turned out to be the highest since 1959.

Amazingly, 1968 showed a short-term improvement. Income exceeded expenses by $16,777. At the end of the year the Council's net worth had gone from a deficit of $7,230 to a positive balance of $9,547. Council President Couden struck a bright note for 1969. He forecast "that our current financial status will allow a continuation of present programs and a limited preoccupation with meeting obligations."

And yet there was a serious lag in church giving. Cash receipts did not measure up to earlier expectations. By September church giving was down $8,000, and individual giving was $1,150 less than what had been budgeted. As a result the Council ended the decade in a precarious financial condition. Though circumstances were different (that is, no large carryover obligations and no heavy support of the state Council), the operating difficulties in the final year of the old Council were not much easier than those of 1959.

Fund-Raising Methodology—During most of the 1960s the Council organized its fund-raising efforts, as had been done in earlier times, on the model of successful YMCAs and other non-profit organizations. Most annual campaigns had tiers of "commanders," "captains," and solicitors, variously named in different years, to solicit both churches and individuals, business firms, and other sources. There was a succession of kickoff luncheons, followed by report meetings (again, often luncheons), and at the conclusion, "victory" celebrations—all at Council expense.

In order to work effectively within the budget-making cycles of different denominational groups, the Council's Church Campaign would generally extend over several months. The Individual Gifts Campaign would have a relatively short span in the fall, often November and December.

In the initial years of the decade there was still an Advance Gifts Campaign to solicit larger contributors. This unit enlisted fairly prominent business, legal, and professional persons as solicitors. In a carryover from the past, the initial kick-off luncheons were held at the Rainier Club. As time went on, the campaign organization and the costs of campaigning were gradually reduced and simplified. At first in somewhat subordinate roles, women came to have an increasingly large part, especially in telephone follow up to "clean up" after campaign solicitors.

Working Toward Primacy of Church Support—A basic principle of the Council has been that it should depend primarily on member churches for its budget support. In that tradition, the provisional constitution of 1961, therefore, stipulated that the Council's financial base should be its member bodies.

The Council inherited the concept of Honor Goals. In 1957 the Council adopted a formula that was being used elsewhere, namely, that the churches' fair-share support of the Council would be two per cent of their current expense and benevolence budgets (but not including building funds or debt retirement).

In 1959, if generally observed, this suggested goal would have brought in more than $91,000. In contrast, contributions from churches and from church-related individuals which could be credited to churches totaled $33,976. At the January 1960 annual meeting, of the 171 churches which received citations for their 1959 contributions, only six were given special mention for reaching or exceeding their two per cent Honor Goals. However, a total of 104 had enlarged their support over the 1958 level.

In the revised constitution of 1966, the Council established a new standard, namely "the proportionate share goal," which was $1 per member. Using this formula in the 1968 Annual Report, twenty-seven congregations/parishes were named as Honor Churches, including seven Roman Catholic parishes. Seven additional denominations were represented.

References have been made to the Seattle Council's financial obligations to the state Council. Although higher amounts had been proposed, the Seattle Council, being somewhat cautious (and yet not entirely realistic) accepted a figure for 1959 of $10,000. Even this amount proved burdensome. Therefore, the Council scaled its 1960 state contribution down to $6,299, and in 1961 to $5,636. Each successive year this amount was reduced. By 1967 and 1968 the Seattle Council contribution to the state was $1,000 each year.

The Trust Fund Concept—Beginning in 1959, occasional contributions were received for special causes that did not come under the authorized budget. Gradually, the concept of "trust and custodial" funds was developed. To formalize this policy, in 1961 the Board approved a new bank account, the "Greater Seattle Council of Churches—Trust Account."

In 1967 a Sustaining and Memorial Fund was launched with a goal of $10,000. It was to be a working reserve to be used during the financially lean summer months. In the Annual Report for 1968 it was announced that the goal had been reached. Fortunately, the settlement of a $6,364 estate provided a large portion of this amount.

Responsibility for Office Facilities—During these years the Council occupied the fourth floor of the Racine Building at 2005 Fifth Avenue in Seattle. When the combined councils moved there (1954), a five-year lease was entered into, which the Seattle Council assumed when the separation took place. Rental costs were shared. In the fall of 1959 after considering the availability and cost of other space, the

Council renewed the lease, and continued to sublease space to the Washington State Council.

In late 1964 after a renewed denominational suggestion for an Interchurch Center proved again to be unrealistic, the Racine Building was leased for another five years. However, at the beginning of 1965 the state Council, hoping to establish more of its own identity, moved to separate facilities in the same building. Fortunately, the Friends of Youth, which had been brought in as a struggling young agency in 1959 on a rent-free basis, signed a lease to occupy part of the state Council's space. In addition, the Seattle Branch of the American Association of University Women came in as an additional tenant on a two-year lease.

Again, in late 1969, the Council faced the end of its lease. It was losing its last co-tenant. Shortly, the Friends of Youth was to move to its newly built Griffin Home in Kennydale. In view of the Council's uncertain future, a six-month extension was granted, allowing the new Church Council administration time to decide what its future needs would be.

An Advisory Role for Denominational Executives

Although without provision in the Council constitution, in late 1963 an important auxiliary body, called Denominational Executives Advisory Committee, started meeting. According to the archives of the Seattle Council, the purposes were: (1) to provide fellowship and exchange on problems and interests of the denominational executives, and (2) to focus largely, at least at first, on the metropolitan Seattle area, and thus to preview and "test" programs of the Greater Seattle Council.

By December 18, 1963, the group had come up with the project called CURE. (See the section above on civil rights). Upon completion of that three-month campaign, during which weekly meetings were held, the executives intended to meet monthly in order to follow up and "give attention to other concerns."

Later an informal, long-standing weekly breakfast group of bishops and other denominational executive leaders began regularly to meet, inclusive then also of Catholic, Episcopal, and Lutheran bishops and increasingly focused on state Council interests. This group continues to this day, now meeting one afternoon a week for those who are able to assemble for fellowship and exchange of ideas and concerns, but with little or no policy or legislative powers. Occasionally, as will be reported later in this Council story, these church leaders have taken on a programmatic leadership role, such as in the 1987 Apology to Native Americans of the Pacific Northwest.

Giving Credit Where Credit Is Due

Naturally, there were many clergy and lay leaders who served as elected Council presidents, vice presidents, and other officers and workers during this period. These persons can be only briefly and inadequately acknowledged here with deepest thanks.

Volunteer Officers—Those who served as president (the incumbent's functions being primarily to preside at important Council meetings, to advise on policy issues, to represent the Council, when requested, at major public events, and to counsel and support the Executive Minister) were:

The Rev. Elmer B. Christie, Church of the Epiphany (Episcopal), Seattle, 1959.

Dr. Paul Raver, Seattle City Light Superintendent and lay leader, University Christian Church, 1960.

The Rev. L. David Cowie, University Presbyterian Church, Seattle, 1961 (first half year).

The Rev. Max W. Morgan, Seattle First Baptist Church, 1961 (last half year) and 1962.

The Rev. Everett J. Jensen, Gethsemane Lutheran Church, Seattle, 1963 and 1964 (first half year).

The Rev. Robert A. Thomas, University Christian Church, Seattle, 1964 (last half year) and 1965.

The Rev. Samuel B. McKinney, Mount Zion Baptist Church, Seattle, 1966 and 1967.

Mr. Elliott N. Couden, realtor, businessman, and lay leader, Fauntleroy Community Church (U.C.C.), Seattle, 1968 and 1969. Due to the leave of absence of the Executive Minister from mid-1968 through 1969, Mr. Couden took on many additional time-consuming responsibilities. He successfully steered the Council through the long process of redesign with its many ambiguities and uncertainties.

In a more complete record the various vice presidents (often women), recording secretaries (almost always women), finance campaign leaders and treasurers (always men), and department chairpersons would be listed with greatest appreciation. Their contributions of time, wisdom, emotional support, and friendship linger long in memory. There would also be mentioned the thousands (two thousand in 1967 alone) of volunteers who served on committees and in program activities.

Employed Staff—Because the employed staff members were always few in number, they carried unusually heavy loads. Day in and day out, year after year, they could be counted on to undertake their work assignments with devotion and enterprise of the highest magnitude.

Those on a full-time executive/professional level were:

> Maude Ricker, a former Methodist missionary and YWCA staff member, who was employed by the Council from 1956 until 1964. She coordinated Christian education, institutional ministry assignments, and several other program responsibilities.
>
> Jessie Kinnear (later Kenton), Presbyterian church staff member, who began in 1961 in finance and business, then increasingly moved into public relations and general operations.
>
> Betty Phillips, a Presbyterian church educator, who served from 1964—1969 as program director of Christian education and other functions.

At various times, there were other persons (named elsewhere in this chapter) who performed professional program assignments on a part-time basis in such functions as armed services ministry, hospital and other institutional chaplaincy coordination, and general social ministries.

Secretaries, bookkeepers, receptionists, and others who provided office skills and labor were also greatly appreciated. Perhaps, because of frequent controversies resulting in harassing phone calls, those whose duties included answering the phone were, in retrospect, most to be valued.

Wrapping It All Up

A full history would also sketch the various controversies and diversions of the period. If a history volume is to be more than a "puff piece," it must confront some of the more unpleasant aspects of an institution or a time period. However, space constraints allow mention here only of the fact that almost constantly, year after year, there was some kind of dissonance on the Council's radar scope. Some of these complaints and objections were merited. No institution is perfect. Others, however, were less justified. The two major themes of such controversy during this decade were fear of "communist infiltration of the churches" (a hold-over from the communist scares of the 1920s and 1930s, renewed by the fears of the Cold War) and the Council's vigorous involvement in the civil rights movement. Like brush fires, there were numerous other controversies of shorter duration on other subjects.

From the vantage point of the *new* Church Council (1970-1995) it may seem that the events, programs, and personalities of previous generations are ancient history. Although sometimes now characterized as "marginal," Council activities in its earlier days were vital to the life and outreach of churches and community.

Certainly, this affirmation is true for the years 1959-1969. It has been the thesis here that this decade was in itself a notable era in the seventy-five-year sweep of Council existence. Officers, staff, and volunteers in large numbers and enthusiastic participation provided the muscle and power for the four significant accomplishments discussed in Chapter V.

Concurrently, there were numerous program activities carried over from the past. Some were allowed to expire, their usefulness having come to an end; others were shifted to other shoulders; a few were maintained essentially as they had existed; and those with promise were expanded for more effective ministry and service.

Amid difficulties and distractions the Council had the good fortune to attempt certain creative projects that held hope for the future. It also was a welcome midwife in helping to bring to life various vital community services. And it found favor in assisting public institutions with a number of their difficult tasks.

The decade of transition was a complex one. It had its frustrations, especially in the realm of finances. But thanks be to God, this intermediate decade also was blessed with many opportunities for creative service to church and community. It was indeed a beacon, even if an inadequate one at times, for the promise that *all may be one…and that all may live in a world of peace, justice, and well-being.*

VII

Launching the New Council, 1970-1978

William B. Cate

THE NEW Church Council of Greater Seattle was born in 1970, and in the first few years significant energy was directed toward "setting a stride" for its operation in the community.

By 1970 metropolitan Seattle was enjoying international acclaim as an important west coast seaport, due in part to the successful 1962 World's Fair. The local economy, however, was dismal because The Boeing Company had fallen on hard times. Since its stellar days during World War II, Boeing had experienced spectacular growth in the commercial airplane business, which, together with military contracts, had caused its employment to soar past one hundred thousand in the late 1960s. Now, in 1970, the company had lost some military contracts, and airlines were not purchasing the new giant 747s as anticipated. By the spring of that year, employment dropped below forty thousand. Economists stated that when Boeing sneezed, Seattle caught a cold. It was true. As a result, one of the first tasks of the new

Church Council was to address issues related to the economic down-turn and its effects on people.

Seattle was blessed with a capable African-American community and had weathered the civil rights struggles of the sixties better than other cities across the country. The Model Cities Program enabled this community to make some changes in open housing and minor-ity empowerment. The leadership of the Seattle African-American community had begun to address other civil rights issues as well, such as quality integrated education, inclusion of people of color in labor unions and the building industry, and relationships between the Af-rican-American community and rapidly growing Asian and Hispanic communities. Seattle continued to face the challenge of integrating these groups into the economic, social and political life of the city.

During the 1960s, Seattle churches had experienced disturbing urban turbulence, but also the promise of Christian unity. Thomas A. Connally, Archbishop of the Roman Catholic Archdiocese of Seattle, had responded positively to the ecumenical thrust of Vatican II, and by 1970, the Roman Catholic Church was an equal partner in the Church Council of Greater Seattle.

Councils of Churches across the country were finding it difficult to respond to problems of the 1970s, such as racism, poverty, and the decline of inner cities. Metropolitan area churches were reluctantly casting off the vestiges of "frontier church" attitudes. The dichotomy between personal salvation and social responsibility, evident in Ameri-can Protestantism for several decades, was no longer a major issue for mainline denominations. The world beyond the four walls of the church was considered a legitimate sphere for the Church's ministry of transformation. Protestant denominations were developing a plan for a new united Church through the Consultation on Church Union, and Christian unity was seen as a possibility for the future. It was into this waiting and potent environment that the Church Council of Greater Seattle was created and prepared for implementation.

The New Ecumenical Creation

A task force chaired by David Colwell, pastor of Plymouth Con-gregational Church, Seattle, designed the new structure. Colwell was responsible for the preamble, having been a United Church of Christ representative to the Consultation on Church Union. The vision of "one Church" which developed out of that ecumenical study process became the theological cornerstone of the Church Council of Greater Seattle. The imperative for this ecumenical instrument was to heal the brokenness of the Church in Seattle, thus allowing it to be an agent of the healing love of God in the world. Unity and justice became the two undergirding values.

The Council would not itself *be* the one Church, but the instrument through which unity among the churches could become a reality. It would play a role as facilitator among separated churches and between the churches and society. It would identify needs in church and community, develop strategies, and mobilize the denominations and congregations to address the needs. The statement of purpose in the constitution reads, "It is the corporate purpose of the Council to be a visible symbol of the Church on the metropolitan level and to carry forward the mission of the Christian Church by providing a structure within which the several denominational judicatories, local congregations, Church-related entities, and certain para-church organizations may make the determinations and decisions necessary to effective witness and ministry in the Greater Seattle area."

The Council would be led by a president-director elected for a five year term as president of the organization as well as the director of the program. The purpose for this departure from the past structure was to give the president-director more ecclesiastical stature—allowing him/her to speak for the Council with more authority in the church and community.

Following a nationwide search, the position was offered to William B. Cate, a United Methodist clergyperson. He had served for twelve years as Executive Director of the Greater Portland Council of Churches in Portland, Oregon, and directed the Interchurch Council of Greater New Bedford, Massachusetts for five years. He had completed a Ph.D. in social ethics and ecumenism, and had authored, *The Ecumenical Scandal On Main Street*, a book about local ecumenism. His mandate was to make the new plan for the Church Council of Greater Seattle a reality.

Cate revealed later that a compelling reason for his accepting the position was his attraction to the theological preamble of the Council's constitution, which set forth the vision for the churches of Greater Seattle as *one* church. The task of the Council was to heal the brokenness in the Church and the brokenness of the world. Church councils up to this time had spoken little of Christian unity, placing more emphasis on interchurch cooperation in social ministry.

A Rough Beginning—At 9:00 A.M. on March 15,1970, William B. Cate sat down at his desk in the fourth floor office of the former Council of Churches of Greater Seattle at Fifth and Virginia in downtown Seattle and looked around at the Council's assets and resources. He had inherited a small staff headed by Jessie Kinnear Kenton who had kept the organization alive in the absence of a director. The annual budget was $69,000, but only $54,000 had been committed. There was little program. Church support had largely collapsed and gifts from businesses and individuals were small and few in number. It was necessary to find cheaper office space immediately.

Cate had been told, when recruited, that denominations would finance the new Church Council. When he arrived in Seattle, he learned that a survey of denominational bodies had been taken in the fall of 1969, and they were not willing to support the new Council. It would be up to the Seattle churches. This was a serious disappointment, but later developments indicated that this may have been providential. Across the nation denominations were cutting back on their support of local church councils, and it was clear that the Church Council would be funded by member congregations and committed individuals, or not at all.

Less expensive office space was found at 314 Fairview Avenue North, near the offices of *The Seattle Times*. This location proved advantageous for the Council, because it was handy for Ray Ruppert, religion editor for the *Times*, to drop in often. If funds were particularly low and a program was in trouble, Ruppert would write a dramatic story on the church page, urging support of the Council so it could continue with some vital program. Ray must be given credit for helping the Church Council through a few hard times.

Not only was raising money going to be difficult, but the "Boeing Downturn" was creating social needs of major proportions in the Greater Seattle area. No existing religious or welfare organization was prepared to handle this situation. Emory Bundy, Director of Community Relations for King-TV, asked William Cate (who had been in Seattle only a few weeks) what he was going to do about the growing problem of hunger in the community. Cate's response was to pull together a group of people including Al Ward, Ecumenical Metropolitan Ministry; Harry Holloway, Vice President of Pacific Northwest Bell Telephone Company; Harold Perry, Director of Fellowship of Christians in Urban Service (FOCUS); and Emory Bundy. Their purpose was to plan for a massive food bank program through the churches. The resulting program, Neighbors in Need, fed hundreds of thousands of hungry people in the community.

A Plan for the Future—A new way of doing ecumenical work was developing. The Council was making an effort to determine the primary mission of the Church in the community, and once determined, to mobilize the energy of the whole Church to carry out the necessary tasks. The Board of the Church Council and the religious community in general agreed that justice issues were the highest priority, and particularly justice for those who were powerless in our society. The Board of Directors established a planning committee in the spring of 1970, and this committee sponsored a program planning conference for June 2, 1970. The conference established priorities for the Council, setting a course for the next twenty years. The needs of the community would shape the kinds and number of programs. The issues that emerged were: (1) minority empowerment; (2) youth (including children and family issues); (3) quality of life (food, housing, education. ecology. etc.); and (4) peace. During the next years, social issues brought to the attention of the Council were considered in light of these priorities. Several major thrusts of the Council's work for the ensuing years are discussed in the following pages.

Racial Justice

Murray Trelease, a canon at St. Mark's Episcopal Cathedral, chaired the Council Planning Committee. The committee's method of operation was to develop the dimensions of each concern. The issue of minority empowerment, for example, was dissected into a number of areas centered around minority oppression by the majority:

Segregation in public housing.

Discrimination in banking, loans and credit.

Lack of power in church structures.

Discrimination in labor unions.

Private club discrimination.

Discrimination in fire and other insurance.

Allocation of funds, public and private and church—including appointment of minorities into decision-making bodies.

Unequal administration of justice and police protection.

Racist curriculum—public schools and church schools.

Discrimination in contract allocation.

Empowerment of minority business.

Each of these items was analyzed carefully regarding the nature of the problem, and an action strategy developed. The absence of minority power in the religious community led to an extensive racial audit of denominational structures. An integrated committee, half of its members Caucasian and half people of color, was chaired by Tsugeo Ikeda and Theodore Bode. The committee developed and administered the audit with no involvement by Council staff. The Church Council itself was also audited. The candid reports they prepared for each church group involved was impressive. The conclusion was that *the Church was racist*. Some of the church leaders became defensive, but the message was clear. In 1972, a caucus of minority Church Council board members requested that the Board meet every two months over a six-month period to discuss nothing but minority-majority relationships. It should be noted here that a similar racial audit was conducted years later when the Council was much larger, and the results were similar.

In private clubs, the issue was state subsidy of discrimination in granting Class H liquor licenses to private clubs which excluded people of color. Churches were urged by the Church Council to ask members to boycott such clubs. On one occasion, William Cate was invited to address a congregation that wanted to hear about the Neighbors In Need food bank program. During the discussion period, the lay presider asked, "What else are you doing in the Council?" Cate told about the effort to eliminate discrimination in private clubs. The presider quickly ended the meeting, and Cate was never invited back to that church.

The Council's concern about racial discrimination in banking led to extensive investigation of "Redlining." Discrimination in education led to a valiant effort by the Council to desegregate Seattle Public Schools.

Empowerment of minority owned business was slow in coming, but found expression later in the 1980s and 1990s through the Black Dollar Days led by Robert Jeffrey, minister of New Hope Missionary Baptist Church.

Tsugeo Ikeda, director of the Atlantic Street Service Center and member of the Planning Committee, suggested that the Council help minority people in United Way agencies become more influential in their own agencies. William Cate called all of the United Way Agency minority board members together for a special caucus. They strategized and encouraged their agencies to become more involved in minority concerns and to increase their hiring of minority staff. The effort was effective, but the Church Council was critized by the United Way for "unethical intrusion into the business of other agencies." Members of minority groups , however, were pleased.

The concern for unequal administration of justice and police protection spoke to an uneasy trust of the police by the people in Seattle's Central Area after an African-American man was shot in the back while fleeing the police. A Police/Community Task Force was established, headed by Carrie Sheehan, a Roman Catholic layperson. The Task Force mediated community concern to the police, not only about police mistreatment of people of color but also people from the gay community.

When Tyree Scott, an African-American contractor, protested racism in labor unions and the construction trades by camping on the lawn of the Federal Court House, the Church Council Board voted to support him and supply him with sandwiches. Later the Council protested when he was jailed unfairly.

Neighbors in Need

As described earlier, the issue of hunger in the Seattle area was addressed because Emory Bundy brought it to the Board, and the result was Council initiation of and involvement in Neighbors in Need. It began as an official program at the Fall Assembly of the Council in 1970. Staff was provided by the Council, FOCUS, and the Ecumenical Metropolitan Ministry to carry on the program. It remained under the Church Council umbrella until it separately incorporated. Even then the Council staff helped in the operation of the program. One of the leaders of Neighbors in Need during these years was Peggy Maze, a Roman Catholic laywoman. The program unfortunately ran into trouble in 1975 when it ill-advisedly entered into an arrangement with William Randolph Hearst, Jr. to distribute three million dollars worth of food to the poor in San Francisco as requested by Patty Hearst's kidnappers. In 1976, as a result of this effort, a legal suit for several million dollars was filed against Neighbors in Need, and the program was forced to disband. The Church Council helped pick up the pieces and designed the Emergency Feeding Program.

Emergency Feeding Program

When the Neighbors In Need program ended, the Planning Committee sought ways to develop a different program to combat hunger in the area. Black Churches felt they had been shut out of Neighbors In Need in 1970, so in order to ensure that this didn't happen again, Black United Clergy For Action (BUCFA) was involved in planning its successor. Mary Lou Beck, an Episcopal lay woman finishing her Masters Degree in nutrition at the University of Washington, had worked in the Neighbors In Need Program. She introduced the idea of an emergency feeding program which would be nutritional and would serve emergency cases referred by social workers and clergy. Special centers for distribution would be placed primarily in strategically located churches. "Crisis Boxes," as they were called, of nutritional food would be donated by local churches to these centers. Content specifications were provided by EFP for people in the churches.

The governing board of the Emergency Feeding Program consisted of twelve members, six appointed by BUCFA, four appointed by the Church Council, and two appointed by Asian Churches. BUCFA would always have administrative control of the program. The first director of the Emergency Feeding Program was Otis J. Moore, pastor of Prince of Peace Baptist Church. Under his leadership the program gathered speed quickly and soon was providing thousands of crisis boxes each month to carefully screened needy people referred by community social agencies and pastors. Moore served as the program's director until his retirement in 1990. What had been expected to be a temporary program, because of the political and social forces of the seventies and eighties continued to serve an undiminished need.

Issues of Peace

The war in Vietnam motivated the Church Council to involve itself in peace issues. In May, 1971, working with Campus Christian Ministry at the University of Washington, the Council sponsored an anti-Vietnam War Rally in Volunteer Park. About fifteen hundred people attended. A small group of African-American bongo drummers had been using the park platform before the peace celebration began. They were reluctant to leave. There were two programs going at the same time for a while—peace speeches and bongo drums. Newspaper reports about the event stated that the neighbors had not appreciated the bongo drumming at the peace rally.

This event led to a September, 1971, decision by the Board of Directors of the Council to organize a Seattle Religious Peace Action Committee (SERPAC), comprised of representatives from all the denominations, the World Without War Council, the Fellowship of Reconciliation and the American Friends Service Committee. Clergy and Laity Concerned about Vietnam, a national religious peace organization, offered a small stipend to SERPAC for staff if SERPAC would agree to be the local area committee for their organization. William Hershey, Lutheran chaplain with Campus Ministry at the University of Washington, gave some time to SERPAC during the first year.

SERPAC organized several Witnesses for Peace called by the bishops, and continued to address peace and human rights issues for the Church Council of Greater Seattle. After the Yom Kippur War in 1973 SERPAC convened a meeting on the subject, "How Is Peace Possible In The Near East?" Speakers were Farhat Ziedeh, a Palestinian-American and chair of the University of Washington's Near East Studies Department and William Greenberg, rabbi of Ezra Bessaroth Synagogue. It was not until twenty-one years later, in 1994, that the Church Council actually established a Task Force on Palestinian Concerns, with Ziedeh as chairperson.

In 1976, Pat Taran of the University Friends Meeting brought to SERPAC his concern for Chilean refugees who were arriving in Seattle after the overthrow of Salvador Allende of Chile by the military forces of General August Pinochet in 1973. SERPAC recommended that the Church Council develop a program to care for Chilean families. The Council worked with Pat Taran and Verne and Genevieve Hathaway from Plymouth Congregational Church to settle over fifty families throughout the city. The Chileans became a part of life in Seattle easily since most of them were skilled tradesmen. They remained close to the Council for years, calling for aid regularly to fight the dictatorship that had seized their country.

Later on in the 1970s it was Pat Taran who also brought to SERPAC the concern for South Africa and its inhuman apartheid system.

Native American Concerns

Puget Sound has its own indigenous human rights problem, the violation of the treaties and rights of Native Americans. Treaties, which Native American peoples were forced to make with the United States as their land and fish were taken from them, were being violated continually by European Americans as if they never existed. In the 1970s, this was brought to the attention of the Church Council of Greater Seattle in a variety of ways:

> Native American tribes were attempting to reclaim the fishing rights granted by the treaties.

> Native Americans were being arrested by the State Game Department as they fished for salmon and steelhead, a right given to them by treaties.

> Several shootings and other incidents of violence on the rivers, lakes and waterways of Puget Sound had received the desired media attention.

> Media attention across the country had been focused on the confrontation between U.S. Marshals/FBI agents and Native Americans at Wounded Knee.

The Church Council of Greater Seattle convened a meeting at Temple De Hirsch on May 23, 1973 with a group of Native Americans, who had asked for a conference to discuss their fishing rights in the Pacific Northwest. This conference led to the establishment of a Native American Task Force, headed by Robert Winkel, a Lutheran pastor. The Task Force spent much of its first year listening to Native American concerns and trying to understand the concept of Native American sovereignty. Most Pacific Northwest European Americans had lived beside Indian people all their lives with little personal contact. Their understanding of Native Americans was at the level of western movies. The Task Force began to view the various tribes as sovereign nations that had been defeated by the United States government. As such, they made treaties with the United States concerning their land, water and resources, and the United States had violated these treaties.

In 1974, George Boldt, a federal judge, interpreted a nineteenth century treaty between the United States Government and the Indian nations to say that all of the fish and resources of Puget Sound were to be held "in common." This phrase, he interpreted, meant fifty-fifty—half for the Indian nations and half for citizens of the United States.

The Boldt Decision was obviously not a popular one with many people. It immediately granted political and economic power to Native Americans in the Puget Sound region. The first act of the Task Force was to support Native American Treaty rights. The Boldt decision was appealed to the U.S. Supreme Court for review. The Task Force lead by Joan La France, a Chippewa Indian woman who worked for the American Friends Service Committee, developed an Amicus Brief from the churches supporting the decision. The United States Supreme Court eventually affirmed the Boldt Decision.

The next stage in the Task Force's life was to play a mediating role between the newly authorized Washington State Native American Fishing Commission and the State Department of Fisheries. They were having difficulty functioning in the same arena. James Dolliver, Administrative Assistant for Governor Daniel Evans, asked Robert Winkel and William Cate to arrange a meeting between Native American leaders, who trusted the Council, and department heads of the State Departments of Fisheries, Game, Finance and the Attorney General's office. The meeting was held at Pacific Lutheran University with Church Council representatives leading the meeting and guiding the discussion. After several hours of often violent accusation and charges and counter charges, the anger of the participants seemed to disappear and the participants began to talk together. When the day was over, some new joint planning had begun. Several years later, at

The Rev. Gertrude L. Apel, center, and the Rev. C.E. Polhemus, Presbyterian Synod Executive, receive a briefing on future developments in the City of Seattle from an official of the City Planning Commission. *1948*
Special Collections, University of Washington Libraries, Neg. #17123

Mrs. Margaret Christie, Episcopal, right, with another leader from the Seattle United Church Women receive used clothing for the Council's United Church Overseas Relief (Church World Service) program at Garfield High School, Seattle. *About 1948.* Special Collections, University of Washington Libraries, Neg. #17118

Council staff member conducts vacation church school at the Yesler Terrace Housing Project. *Late 1940s.* Special Collections, University of Washington Libraries, Neg. #17122

Council of Churches Hostess House. Service men receive help from a volunteer of the Seattle United Church Women. *Probably late 1940s.*
Special Collections, University of Washington Libraries, Neg. #17036

Council staff appear with the new mobile chapel for the state-wide migrant ministry work. Left to right: The Rev. Chester Ramsey, The Rev. Gertrude L. Apel, Kaoru Ichihara, Andrea Olsen, Lu Apel Henderson, and Mrs. Harry Slick. *1950*
Special Collections, University of Washington Libraries, Neg. #17120

Christian Pavilion and Children's Center at the Seattle World's Fair, April 22 - October 21, 1962, which provided Christian educational child care to Fair visitors, a short motion picture presentation on the biblical themes of Creation, Redemption, and Consummation, a meditation chapel, two major Christian art works, and a gift shop with appropriate biblical and Christian souvenirs.
Special Collections, University of Washington Libraries, Neg. #17117

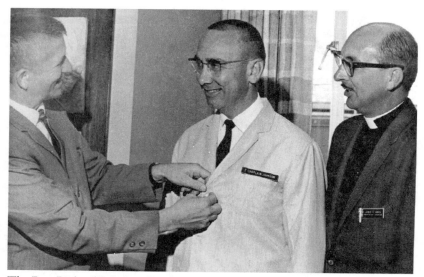

The Rev. Richard Johnson, Presbyterian, is greeted by the Swedish Hospital Administrator upon Johnson's assignment as full-time Swedish Hospital Chaplain. The Rev. James Vance, Evangelical United Brethren/United Methodist pastor, serving as the Council's part-time Coordinating Chaplain, helps to make arrangements for all such institutional ministries. *1965.*

Special Collections, University of Washington Libraries, Neg. #17126

Four Seattle area bishops prepare to participate in the memorable second annual Public Gathering of Prayer for Christian Unity, held January 23, 1966, in the Seattle Center Arena. Left to right: Episcopal Bishop Ivol Ira Curtis, Methodist Bishop Everett W. Palmer, Catholic Archbishop Thomas A. Connolly, and Catholic Auxiliary Bishop Thomas Gill (all deceased).

Special Collections, University of Washington Libraries, Neg. #17125

Robert A. Thomas, President, 1964-1965, turns over Council duties to in-coming President Samuel B. McKinney, 1966-1967.

First session of Ministers Institute on Youth Problems, November 15, 1960, King County Juvenile Court and Youth Center. Left to right: The Rev. Lemuel Petersen, Edd Crawford, Robert Utter.

The Rev. Samuel B. McKinney, Baptist pastor and Council president-elect, is at the podium of the Public Gathering for Christian Unity, January 23, 1966, Seattle Center Arena. The Rev. Lemuel Petersen, Executive Minister, is at the extreme right. The Sanctuary Choir of the Seattle First Methodist Church provides the liturgical music.

92

Raymond G. Hunt-
hausen, Archbishop of
the Diocese of Seattle,
speaking at one of many
peace rallies.

The Rev. David G.
Colwell, Minister Emeri-
tus of Plymouth Congre-
gational Church below.

Timothy Nakayama, rector of St.
Peter's Episcopal Church, who
served the Council as Vice President
and cochaired with Cynthia
Domingo the Asia Pacific Task
Force.

Ted George, a prominent Native American Leader, who served on the Native American Task Force of the Council, speaking at William Cate's retirement banquet in 1990.

Patrinell Wright, frequent leader of gospel music concerts for the Council.

Arthur Lee, director of the Emergency Feeding Program with some of his staff.

94

Charles Meconis, a director of
SERPAC.

Jonathan Nelson, (above right) Lutheran pastor, member of the Seattle Ecumenical Religious Peace Action Coalition standing before his boat USS Plowshares which was used in the peace blockade of the nuclear submarine USS Ohio.

Plowshares carrying his crew, which included his mother, at a peace demonstration on August 11, 1982. Photo by Loren Arnett

Robert Jeffrey, pastor of New Hope Baptist Church, organizer of Black Dollar Days.

Barbara Hurst, director of the Seattle area American Jewish Committee and Farhat Ziedeh, chair of the Council's Palestinian Concerns Task Force.

Imo Steele, the epitome of volunteerism, who served with many other lay volunteers in office tasks.

Donald Daughtery served as chair of the Racial Justice in Education Task Force in its beginning.

Tyna Fields, a vice-president of the Council and first and long-term chair of the South Africa Task Force.

Patriarch Aleksiy II of the Russian Orthodox Church inspecting the Council's printing press during his visit to Seattle in 1989 while still Metropolitan of Leningrad.

Robert Winkel, a Lutheran pastor, organizing chair of the Native American Task Force, who served several crucial years as the chair of the Council Planning Committee.

Terri Ward, who served several years as Youth Service Center Chaplain.

Mary Liz Chaffee, staff person for the Task Force on Aging.

Since the late 1970s, the Rev. David Bloom, Associate Director for Urban Ministry, has led the development of the Council's substantial urban programs in such areas as housing, homelessness, children and youth, labor relations and racial justice.

Joseph Martin who served as chair of the Mental Health Task Force and supported John Fox and David Bloom in inner city housing concerns.

William Cate with Richard Spady, a volunteer for the Council for twenty years, undertaking pioneer efforts in fast forum feedback communication.

The Source staff and production crew caught in a lighter moment after the paper went to press. Standing (left to right) Grant Angle, Ad Manager; Marge Lueders, Editor-in-Chief; Victoria Campbell and June Click, feature writers. Seated: Lyndol Pullen, Source Advisory Board and Joan Reed, Associate Editor.

Esther "Little Dove" John, founder and director of the Mission for Music and Healing Task Force.

David Aasen, Minister of the First United Methodist Church of Seattle, who in myriad ways supported the ministry of the Church Council of Greater Seattle.

Sharehouse workers deliver furniture to those in need.

Partners for Peace Walk participants: Ellis Carson, First AME Church, Mayor Norman Rice, Anthony Robinson, Plymouth Congregational Church, Elaine Stanovsky, Director CCGS, Samuel B. McKinney, Mt. Zion Baptist Church.

Orie Green, Council secretary and member of Grace United Methodist Church.

Josephine Archuleta, Director of the Homeless Action Network.

Palm Sunday March for Archbishop Romero.

Alice Woldt, Associate Director of Administation for the Church Council of Greater Seattle.

Rodney Romney, Minister of the First Baptist Church of Seattle and Vice-President of the Church Coucil.

Leaders at the Desert Storm War Protest March and Service at St. Mark's Episcopal Cathedral: Norman Hirsh, Rabbi Beth Am; Elaine Stanovsky, Director of CCGS; Fredrick Northup, Dean St. Mark's; Archbishop Raymond G. Hunthausen; Ismail Ahmad, Islamic leader; and Sister Kathleen Pruitt.

a meeting with the Native American Task Force and denominational leaders, Ron Schmitten, head of the State Department of Fisheries, and Billy Frank. head of Northwest Indian Fisheries, expressed gratitude for that first meeting and for Council support for their work together.

Homosexuality

The Council faced a new challenge in 1974 when the Metropolitan Community Church (MCC), a mostly Gay and Lesbian congregation, applied for membership. MCC was growing rapidly at this time because people wanted to be open about their homosexual orientation and felt they could not do so and be accepted in most churches. It was the responsibility of the Membership Committee, chaired by Bruce Parker, a United Methodist clergyperson, to examine requests for membership and make recommendations to the Board. Before making a recommendation about the Metropolitan Community Church, they took time to study the issue and to seek input from Council delegates from various denominations. They found that most denominations had not dealt with the issue of homosexuality. After a year of study, the Committee voted (5-2) to recommend admission of the Metropolitan Community Church to the Church Council. They had found that MCC was part of a denomination which adhered to an evangelical statement of faith and that the sexual orientation of its members was irrelevant.

The Board of Directors accepted the recommendation of the Membership Committee with only one dissenting vote. King-TV News was present and televised the entire discussion. At one lighter moment during the proceedings, Board member Edward Hogan, a Roman Catholic priest, said to the Protestants present reflecting on the acceptance of the MCC as a church, "You know, if we Catholics had had the opportunity to vote you Protestants into the Church you never would have made it." Orthodox Jewish Rabbi, Arthur Jacobowitz, responded, "That's right, Father!"

This action was only the beginning of the Church Council's involvement with the issue of homosexuality. A task force was set up in May, 1976, to educate within the Church Council itself, and then the churches. Expecting some obscure name for the task force, the Board was surprised when the group called itself the Lesbian and Gay Men

Task Force of the Church Council of Greater Seattle. Its membership was composed of fifty percent gay and fifty percent straight, and was chaired by an American Baptist woman, Cherry Johnson. Members of the Task Force began by educating themselves and then the Council and member churches about the sociological as well as the theological and biblical concerns involved in the issue of homosexuality.

The fall assembly of the Council in 1976 was a watershed event in this educational process. Margaret Farley, a Roman Catholic Sister and Professor of Social Ethics at Yale Divinity School, spoke on the topic, "Changing Times: the Church and Homosexuality." She traced the history of biblical and ecclesiological teachings about sex, arguing that there are no clear teachings about homosexuality in the Scriptures. It is an issue that we must clarify for the church today, according to Dr. Farley. There were 325 delegates present that Sunday afternoon, plus fifty additional people who identified themselves as gay. Conversation around the tables during the discussions between gay and straight people was intense. Many people among those present stated later that education of the Church Council delegates took a gigantic step forward, and led to a significant change of attitude toward gay and lesbian people in Seattle area churches.

This educational process was disrupted in the fall of 1978, when a national campaign *against* gay rights reached Seattle in the form of a local initiative 13. This national campaign had been initiated by celebrity Anita Bryant, a popular nationally known singer, and had been successful in rescinding homosexual housing and employment rights previously voted in many communities across the nation. With local sponsors the initiative was ready to take Seattle by storm. Seattle's gay community immediately responded. The Church Council Lesbian and Gay Men Task Force led by Cherry Johnson, Marie Fortune and staffed by Pearl McElheran mobilized the religious community and especially the mainline Christian churches against Initiative 13. It was not even a close vote. The initiative was defeated by a two to one margin.

The mainline Christian community and the Jewish religious community had established a strong consensus. There was a committee of prominent community leaders who also opposed the initiative, but the Church Council was the only large community organization outside the gay groups that opposed the measure. Significant to note here is that the Anita Bryant campaign "ran out of gas" in Seattle.

Women's Issues

The role of women in the church, and in our culture generally, was a justice issue that could no longer be ignored. In the newly organized Church Council in 1970, there were only four women on the Board of Directors, one of whom was the President of Seattle Church Women United. Furthermore, this did not seem to bother anyone; it was "normal" for the Church. Throughout its history, the Church had been dominated by men.

In 1972, an interfaith task force of religious women was organized by the National Organization of Women. The group later became independent and called itself the Coalition on Women and Religion and asked to be related to the Church Council as an independent movement. From that position it could seek to make the Church more aware of its treatment of women. It had as its goal to bring women into equal participation with men in the life of the Church and to end the patriarchal dominance of men. Jessie Kinnear Kenton, an associate Council staff person, was a key leader in the Women's Coalition.

A group of five women came to one of the meetings of the Board of Directors of the Council to discuss a possible relationship to the Council. When it was time for them to speak, the President-Director said to them, "Who is your chair*man*?" They were immediately aware of the difficulty of their task.

The Coalition developed a major paper, "A Matter of Justice," which was presented to the Church Council Board by Diana Bader, a Roman Catholic Dominican Sister, later to become a vice president of the Council. This paper demanded that (1) the Church Council seek to have one third of its Board members women; (2) the Council set special sessions of the Board for dialogue with women about their role in the Church; (3) the Council become more sensitive to inclusive language; and (4) the Council create a Task Force on Women and Religion to help implement these goals.

The Women and Religion Task Force was established in 1974. Its chairperson was Sue Wallace. Marie Van Bronkhorst was the part-time staff. That same year, for the first time, the planning committee's priority on justice included women's human rights. The task force led the Board in a consciousness-raising session at its meeting in May, 1975, "to help the Board in its understanding of women and the Church and the cultural revolution that is presently taking place as women struggle for equality." A few more women were elected to the Board in 1975 (21%). The Board voted to support the Equal Rights Amendment to the United States Constitution. They further set a goal of fifty percent women on the Church Council Board of Directors.

The educational thrust of the Women and Religion Task Force was called "Project: Woman's Search." It sought to explore new meanings for women's spirituality, new directions for women in ministry, to celebrate the future of women, and affirm the female dimension of life in the church and the world. Groups of women were organized to carry out this program. Another thrust of the program was "Women Speak," which encouraged churches to celebrate Women Speak Sunday. One year women filled 125 pulpits in the Seattle area. The Women and Religion Task Force became a part of a World Council of Churches study of the "New Community of Women and Men in the Church," the first and only grassroots up faith and order study conference organized by the WCC.

The Church Council of Greater Seattle was one of six metropolitan area Councils worldwide included in this study of new roles for women and men in the Church. Locally, the Task Force worked for many years to heighten the awareness of churches and the Church Council to the changing role of women in the Church. Information in *The Source*, the Council's newspaper, was important. The women were given space, at least one-eighth of the paper without interference by the *Source* Board, to print what they considered consciousness-raising articles concerning human rights of women. By 1980, membership of the Church Council Board was fifty percent women. Women's ordination had increased dramatically in several denominations.

State Lottery and Gambling

The Church Council of Greater Seattle was opposed to a state lottery, stating at its Board meeting on February 12, 1974, that "lottery is a well developed tendency to push the tax burden on those at the lowest end of the economic ladder." The Council had opposed the legalization of pull tabs and punch board gambling in the 1970s as it had in the 1960s, arguing that it leads to the corruption of law enforcement agencies.

By 1990, however, the Seattle City Council legalized pull tabs and punch boards and the state established a state lottery. Indian tribes now have casinos on their reservations.

Boycotts

Because of what they determined were oppressive labor practices, the Church Council supported the national J.P. Stevens boycott in 1977. They also supported the unionization of farm workers by urging church people to participate in a national grape boycott. This ultimately led to the organization of the United Farm Workers. The Council joined the drive to take the state sales tax off of food in 1978. All of these efforts were understood as being done in behalf of powerless people in our society.

A new way of doing conciliar work was developing. Instead of simply doing a few marginal tasks that could be best done ecumenically, what was happening was a concentrated effort to project the mission of the Church *for our time in this place*. Once determined, the Council began to mobilize the energy of the Church to carry out the task. Justice for all people had become the number one priority of the churches, and focus of the Council's energies.

Pastoral Care and Nurturing Ministries

The role of the Church Council of Greater Seattle in justice issues consumed much energy and received considerable public attention because it was often controversial. Pastoral and nurturing ministries, by contrast, were done without fanfare but played an important role in the life of the Council.

Hospital Chaplaincy—Hospital Chaplaincy had a long history in the Church Council. George McCleave, a retired Presbyterian minister, served several years on behalf of the Church Council as coordinator of volunteer chaplains at many of the hospitals in metropolitan Seattle. Richard Johnson, Chaplain at Swedish Hospital, conducted annual pastoral care training for clergy and also laity. Many pastors and laypersons attended these sessions. Early in the 1970s, the

Council's Pastoral Care Committee, chaired by Chaplain Johnson, recommended that hospitals should be encouraged to hire their own chaplains instead of asking denominations to supply the funds for this ministry. Swedish hospital was the only major hospital helping to pay for chaplaincy care. At first, Johnson's salary was paid for by the Seattle Presbytery. Later the hospital began to pick up the cost. At a meeting attended by hospital executives and denominational leaders, the need for funding was explored. This set the stage for hospitals to employ their own chaplains.

Friend to Friend—Joe Rust, a member of St. Philomena's Roman Catholic Church in Des Moines came to the Church Council office in the spring of 1974 to express concern for the forgotten and neglected people in nursing homes. His research had revealed that at that time there were at least twelve thousand people in Seattle area nursing homes, many of whom had no family and friends. Joe's plan was simple and direct. Tell the story of need and then recruit, train and support lay people to be friends to the lonely people in nursing homes. The first effort began in the Des Moines area, and the response was dramatic. Volunteers and money flowed in. The ministry was called "Friend to Friend," and Joe Rust was the coordinator. Through the years that followed the program fluctuated between five hundred and one thousand volunteer "friends" in nursing homes.

Once again, while many justice issues which the Council addressed tended to polarize people, Friend to Friend attracted people from a broad cross section of the church community. Before long the idea spread throughout the Puget Sound region and other states. An important side benefit was the relationship provided between the nursing home community and the Church.

Community Based Correction and Care—Another pastoral care effort beginning at about this time seemed to have great promise, but did not survive. The trend of the early 1970s was to remove people who were incarcerated or mentally ill from large institutions and develop community based programs for their care. In May 1974, Ray Malonson, a former Franciscan priest, came to the Council with an idea for community-based chaplaincy for incarcerated people in these local facilities. A grant was received from the Weyerhauser Timber Company in 1975 to try such a program for one year. The mood of the state that year, however, was becoming more punitive toward people in prison, and Malonson spent considerable time opposing an effort to reintroduce the death penalty into the state of Washington. With no more money for his project, and the growing punitive mood in the state, Malonson decided it was not a good time to pursue his ministry.

Mental Health Chaplaincy—Sometime later the Council addressed the mental health situation in the Seattle area. Joe Pickering, Director of Eastside Mental Health Clinic, was the first chairperson of a task force to study the growing mentally ill population in the Seattle area. Later Joe Martin, a downtown Seattle worker with the poor and elderly, assumed the role. Their concern was for people who had been released from state mental institutions for community-based treatment without any supporting funds to develop and maintain the facilities and programs. In these first years, the primary role of the Council was education and advocacy. It was not until over ten years later that the Council could develop the resources for a mental health chaplaincy program with the Rev. Craig Rennebohm as chaplain.

Youth Center Chaplaincy—The need for a chaplaincy program at the King County Youth Detention Center was brought to the attention of the Church Council from many directions. Such a program began to take shape when Michael Holland, pastor of Immaculate Conception Roman Catholic Church, offered to coordinate a crew of volunteer pastors to work as chaplains at the Youth Service Center. The Youth Service Center had a bad experience with some clergy in the past and was skeptical of the Council's motives. After some months of assurances from the Council, the program was accepted, and soon grew to involve more time than volunteers could give. Howard Robinson, an American Baptist minister, became the Council's first Youth Service Center Chaplain and served until late in the 1980s. He was followed by Terri Ward, a theologically educated Roman Catholic layperson. Churches raised the money for the chaplaincy program because the state could not provide funds for religious activities. The Youth Chaplaincy Program was, and remains, a vital program of the Church Council.

Other Community Needs

During the formative years of the new Church Council, attention was given to many important community needs:

The Drama Committee, headed by Paul Sanford, produced inspirational plays for the Church community.

Celebration of the Bicentennial in 1976, entitled "A New Birth of Freedom."

The Council's effort to look at value education.

Concerns of families and the elderly.

An employment project.

A task force focused on the crisis in Northern Ireland, a concern Ann Williams Bush later related to in behalf of the Council.

Some of these concerns surfaced again in the 1980s and were developed more thoroughly; others were of short duration, meeting a specific need at a particular time.

VIII

A Mature Church Council, 1978-1985

William B. Cate

ISSUES were coming to the attention of the Church Council at an accelerated pace in the late 1970s. The "new" Council was just a few years old, but was operating in a different setting than at the beginning of the decade. It seemed a good time to examine some internal matters, as well as assess the Council's relationship with churches, the community and the world.

Jimmy Carter was President of the United States. The country was still reeling from Watergate, and the Vietnam War was a bitter memory. The great peace concern of the day centered around the fear of a nuclear holocaust resulting from the continuing tensions between the communist East and the capitalist West. Ronald Reagan became President of the United States in 1981 on the wave of the new right, especially the religious right. The Church's commitment to work for justice for all, to feed the hungry and give priority to the poor and the powerless was directly challenged by the newly elected political leaders. It seemed the tide had turned, and the poor again were becoming poorer and the rich were becoming richer.

Jay Lintner, regional staff for the United Church of Christ, proph-
esied that we were about to experience the biggest "rip-off" of the
government and of the people by the wealthy in our history. Racial
justice was put on hold, and people of color were seen as undeserv-
ing. It was said that they had already received more consideration than
they deserved. Mainline Christian churches were being challenged by
the new religious right who had suddenly discovered the political
dimension of our society.

The Seattle area had a long history of being politically liberal. The
city was heterogeneous in race. There were at least fifty thousand gay
people. Seattle's population was quite young. Boeing had begun to
rebuild itself after the calamity of the early seventies. William Gates
Jr. had not yet dropped out of Harvard to create Microsoft, but the
eastside suburbs were already developing new high tech industry. The
Seattle area's economic life was becoming healthy again. Through the
Port of Seattle trade with the Far East was thriving.

Meanwhile, the role of the Church Council as a vehicle for Christian unity had become clearer. Regional denominational leaders and
local congregations were more and more accepting of its coalescing
role in the religious community. They supported Council efforts in
issues of justice and peace which strengthened its witness to the community at large. People could see the positive effects of Christian unity.

Interfaith Concerns

The population of the area was becoming increasingly diverse.
Immigrants from the Pacific Rim and the Middle East, together with
large numbers of people from Southeast Asia, represented different
world religions such as Buddhism, Hinduism and Islam. This, together with an already growing Jewish population, made Seattle more
religiously cosmopolitan than it had been before.

The Church Council was challenged to expand its thinking from
interchurch to *interfaith*. This had actually begun some years earlier
when Peter Schnurman, Director of the American Jewish Committee, had asked that the Jewish community be represented by "official
observers" on the Board of the Church Council. Since the Council
was a Christian body, it was decided that the "observers" would have
full voice at Board meetings but no vote. This status was subsequently

granted to Unitarians, the Bahai Faith, the Vedanta Society and other religious groups. Peter Raible, pastor of the University Unitarian Church, had approached the Board of Directors of the Church Council of Greater Seattle at one point to suggest that the Church Council become an Interfaith Council. The Council explored the idea but has remained officially a Christian body. Several years later, the term, "Observer," was changed to "Interfaith Partner."

The Church of Armageddon—One of the most significant tests of the Church Council's understanding of itself occurred when Serious Israel from the Church of Armageddon, known as the Love Israel Family, asked to join the Council. Most people in the Christian community and in the larger community thought of this group as a "hippy" religious cult whose leader was a man by the name of Love Israel. All members had taken Israel as their last name; and their first names (Serious, Meekness, Charity, etc.) reflected each individual's character. They owned property on Queen Anne Hill, a fishing boat, and a farm near Arlington, Washington. They built or reconstructed their own communal homes and shared everything in common—modeling after the early Christian communities described in the Acts of the Apostles.

The challenge of deciding whether or not to admit this "church" to the Council was given to the membership committee led by James Fairbrook, a United Church of Christ pastor. The committee visited with the Love Israel family, which at that time numbered about 150 members, including children. Love Israel was invited to meet with the Church Council Board of Directors. Finally, the Board decided to admit the Church of Armageddon as an "Official Observer." This was agreeable to the "family," and they appointed two representatives to the Council, Meekness and Softness Israel. They faithfully attended meetings for several years. One member of the Church of Armageddon was the son of celebrity Steve Allen. It was arranged for Steve Allen to do a benefit program for the Church Council on January 24th, 1982. A combo from the Love Israel Family played that evening, and members of the Family served as ushers. They had been accepted into the life of the Council.

In the late 1980s there was a split in the Church of Armageddon over authority in the Church. It was the members who had worked with the Council and its democratic ways who withdrew from the group. The remaining group moved to the farm in Arlington where they still live. They discontinued their relationship with the Church Council when they moved from the city.

The Church Council later developed criteria for considering religious groups for admission as Interfaith Partners. It was felt that groups should share the Council's goals of peace and justice and be willing to work for their causes in the community. Interfaith work was becoming very much a part of the Church Council's agenda. Formation of an Interfaith Council in the late 1980s is discussed later in this narrative.

Communication with Churches and the Community

In the late 1970s, less and less space was given to "church news" in the secular media. The Council established a Leadership Education Task Force to study the situation and make recommendations to the Board of Directors. The Task Force suggested that the Church Council publish and distribute an ecumenical religious newspaper to inform congregations about news of the Church Council and the churches in the area. This would help establish linkages among church members around particular issues. One of the roles of the Church Council was to be a vehicle of communication, coordination and mobilization of churches, and it must have a vehicle for this purpose.

The Source became the official newspaper of the Church Council, the first of its kind in the nation. It has won national recognition, and other Councils of Churches have since established their own newspapers. Doris Warbington and Jessie Kinnear should be named as creators of *The Source*. Jan Cate was established as editor of the monthly which allowed two pages for women's concerns. Later Marge Lueders agreed to be the editor, and with the able assistance of Joan Reed, continues in that role to the present time.

Another important communication technique employed through the years was the *Fast Forum*, developed by Richard Spady, an active Church Council volunteer and supporter. Richard Spady said that no organization or society can be healthy unless it has a feedback system that provides grassroots participation and feedback. Regularly through the years, the Council has used the *Fast Forum* method to evaluate the direction its program was taking. Spady claims that leaders can lead only if they keep in close touch with the opinions of the people they are chosen to lead. The Church Council has tried to be the vehicle to expedite two-way communication in the life of the Church of Greater Seattle. The *Fast Forum* has helped this to happen. Richard Spady served as volunteer staff to the Council for nearly twenty years.

Church Service Agency—As the number of task forces grew, the core staff was more and more involved in bookkeeping functions, audits, and maintenance of records in keeping with Internal Revenue Service regulations. This service was necessary for the health and effectiveness of the Council. The Council became the clearinghouse for money raised by task forces, which amounts to many times more than the core budget. Material was printed and distributed for various programs, and the Council maintained liability insurance and employee benefits for them. Each program paid a small percentage of its gross for these services. This method of operation has continued through the years.

Peace and Justice Issues

Through the years, many groups of people have come to the Church Council with concerns and have asked for assistance getting started or accomplishing their tasks. If the Board felt that the purposes of these groups met Council criteria, they were allowed to operate under the "umbrella" of the Council. Some programs were of short duration and disbanded after the particular task was finished, others started with the Council and later became independent organizations, and others became more permanent Council programs.

A discussion follows about important peace and justice issues involving the Church Council of Greater Seattle during the late 1970s and through the 1980s.

Redlining

Redlining occurs when lending institutions in cities in effect draw a red line around declining inner city areas refusing them credit. Where there is no credit provided in a neighborhood, there is no hope. The people redlined were primarily people of color, poor people in declining neighborhoods, the elderly and single women. Therefore, it was natural that in Seattle the impetus against redlining came from the clergy of Black churches and the Central Seattle Community

Council. The latter provided the staff for the effort. The group asked the Church Council to become a part of the coalition opposing redlining. The Council agreed and Timothy Nakayama, priest of St. Peter's Episcopal Church, was appointed to serve as its representative.

Meanwhile, the City of Seattle had authorized a study to examine the practices of local banks. The study committee had hired Darel Grothaus, a United Methodist clergyperson from the Chicago area, to direct the study. In the meantime, the central area based citizen coalition suffered a severe setback when the two young men who staffed the coalition died in a traffic accident. As a result, most of the responsibility for dealing with the City Council Redlining Committee fell upon the Church Council's Redlining Task Force headed by Timothy Nakayama. The city's committee recommended some new guidelines for banks to follow in order to rectify the redlining situation, and some banks, such as Seattle First National, seemed eager to comply. Darel Grothaus felt churches could play a significant role, and he suggested strategies to the Council task force for making sure that banks would follow through on the new guidelines.

At the suggestion of the Church Council Redlining Task Force the bishops and denominational executives of the Seattle area called a breakfast meeting for clergy at the First African Methodist Episcopal Church on May 27, 1976. As a result of this meeting Timothy Nakayama drafted an impassioned letter to bank presidents in the Seattle area. The letter spoke graphically of bankers who live in great modern glass palaces and who meet in dark places behind closed doors doing their work secretly. He quoted a verse to this effect from John's Gospel. It was a dramatic piece. It pointed out clearly the evil of redlining. Many bishops and denominational executives signed the letter, as well as 150 clergy from many denominations. The letter was so compelling that one corporate leader could quote it years later. It effectively pulled the underpinnings from the rationalizations the bankers were using to justify redlining practices.

The Redlining Task Force kept the pressure on through meetings with bankers individually and in groups, and would invite the press to some of these meetings. Michael Berry, president of Seattle First National Bank, asked to come to the Church Council Fall Delegate Assembly in September, 1976, where he spoke convincingly about the institution's commitment to neighborhood rehabilitation. Darel Grothaus was the featured preacher that evening and spoke prophetically about justice in the city. The Church Council had made its point to the community about redlining and the issue was settled for many years to come. The new policy was stated clearly by the city's Reinvestment Task Force: "Lenders should make loans for the purchase and rehabilitation of houses and apartment buildings on every Seattle block on the same terms as such loans are available in the suburbs, subject only to the credit worthiness of the borrowers and the physical condition of the structure."

Desegregation of Public Schools

As a result of the Supreme Court Brown vs. Board of Education case of 1954, the focus of school desegregation efforts across the country in the late 1950s and 1960s had been on segregation *laws*, especially in the South. A more subtle segregation existed in northern cities. Schools were effectively segregated by *living patterns*, and school systems were run by the dominant "white" culture.

Seattle Public Schools did not employ a black teacher until the 1950s. An effort was made to desegregate Seattle schools voluntarily in the 1960s, and as previously stated in this book, the Church Council had been supportive of the effort. The burden of movement to achieve integration, however, was on the minority families. Few white children were sent to minority schools.

From the first planning conference of the new Church Council of Greater Seattle in 1970, quality education and integrated schools was considered a quality of life, and therefore a justice issue. A task force had been set up, headed by David Colwell, pastor of Plymouth Congregational Church, who later chaired a city-wide council on quality education. Nothing of substance came from this effort except to identify some key players for the later school desegregation effort.

Donald Daughtery, pastor of Beacon Avenue United Church of Christ, brought new energy to the Council on the school desegregation issue in 1976. A task force, Racial Justice in Education, was formed, chaired jointly by Daughtery and Peter Jamero, a Roman Catholic layperson. The group's purpose was to study the issue, hold educational briefings with media, educate the churches and to influence the school administration and the school board. A mission statement entitled, "A New Vision of Racial Justice in Education" was developed which galvanized the task force and many church leaders to desegregate Seattle schools.

The statement was approved by the Board of Directors of the Church Council, a caucus of African-American churches, a caucus of Asian Churches and regional denominational leaders. It was presented to the Seattle School Board in December 1976 and proved to be the Church Council's "school desegregation manifesto," stating the criteria necessary for any acceptable school desegregation plan:

1. It must provide equity for all children.

2. It must affirm that the distinctive priority of public schools is quality education.

3. It must exercise sensitive and flexible judgment in the area of ethnic heritage.

4. More attention must be paid to the fundamental causes of residential segregation in our community.

5. The school administration and the School Board must be entirely open with citizens in planning for desegregation and for equitable and effective education.

Most of the denominational leaders were present at the meeting to support this document, and it precipitated community-wide discussion about school desegregation for months to come. The initiative taken by the Church Council served to shape that discussion.

At this crucial time it was necessary for Donald Daughtery and Peter Jamero to leave the Seattle area because of their employment. David Colwell, pastor of Plymouth Congregational, and Cecil Murray, pastor of First African Methodist Episcopal Church of Seattle, agreed to co-chair the Racial Justice in Education Task Force. Ann Siqueland, a Lutheran layperson and long time activist, served as volunteer staff in the beginning. She conducted educational programs with congregations and helped to develop and implement the actual desegregation plan for the Seattle public schools.

During 1977, the Seattle School Board began talking about magnet schools and seemed to be afraid to "bite the bullet" of mandatory desegregation. The Church Council felt that a voluntary plan had *not* worked in the 1960s and was unlikely to work ten years later. Equity for children must be at the center of any desegregation plan, and there must be a willingness to take mandatory measures to achieve this.

By mid-1970, many community groups were heatedly discussing whether Seattle should voluntarily desegregate its schools or wait for a court order. The Church Council agreed to join with the ACLU and NAACP in a lawsuit forcing the School Board to act. Some other groups, such as the Chamber of Commerce, Municipal League and the Urban League, feared a lawsuit and urged the School Board to lay plans immediately for desegregation of schools. Wesley Uhlman, mayor of Seattle, placed the power of his office behind this request. At its meeting on June 8, 1977, the Seattle School Board approved a timetable and process to rectify racial imbalance in schools. Citizen input would be solicited, and a plan would be presented by December 15, 1977. With significant citizen participation, and especially the effort of Ann Siqueland in behalf of the Church Council, a plan was prepared and adopted in January, 1978.

The Church Council received a grant from the Ford Foundation to help prepare the community for the beginning of the new Seattle plan for school desegregation in September of 1978. Other cities across the country had experienced violence when school desegregation plans were implemented, and Seattle was prepared for this. Desegregation proceeded without violence, however, and without a court order. Changes in the original plan have been made during the years following, but the Church Council of Greater Seattle had played a key role in this historic step toward racial equality in education.

Ann Siqueland worked for the Council another two years to help make the plan operational and to write a book documenting the entire episode, *Without A Court Order: The Desegregation Of Seattle's Schools* (Seattle, Madrona Press, 1981).

Ecology

Care of the earth was raised as a concern in the 1970s when Paul Gertmenian, Presbyterian Campus Minister at the Campus Christian Ministry at the University of Washington, read a thoughtful paper on theology and ecology at a Church Council meeting. The Ecology Task Force, chaired by Robert Schindler, was formed to respond to ecology concerns, and its first effort was the development of a statement on ecology and economics for the Church Council. This statement placed a strong emphasis on the biblical concept of stewardship.

When an oil shortage developed in the decade, the focus of the Ecology Task Force became sources of energy. Nuclear energy seemed to be considered an answer to the scarcity of oil. The Council sponsored a consultation at the University Christian Church in April, 1976, to discuss the matter of nuclear energy. Speakers included experts from the University of Washington and the Northwest Federal Energy Commission. This was followed by a panel consisting of Jay Lintner, clergyperson, Robert Holloran, nuclear engineer, David Ortman, a Mennonite and representative of the Friends of the Earth. The panel discussed ethical issues involved with the use of nuclear energy.

Robert Holloran followed Schindler as chair of the Ecology Task Force, and conservation of energy became its focus. A program to help churches become more energy efficient was developed in partnership with Puget Power and Light Company. This program was widely used and appreciated by the churches. In the mid 1980s the Ecology Task Force became the Ecology and Theology Task Force seeking to raise the consciousness of congregations about their responsibility for stewardship of the earth.

Issues of Peace

The Seattle Religious Peace Action Task Force (SERPAC), had been working closely with local denominational heads on peace and human rights issues around the world. Lauren Friesen, a Mennonite clergyperson, served as SERPAC's staff. During this time, in cooperation with the Washington Commission for the Humanities, SERPAC developed a "Forum on Religious Values and Government Policy," inviting nationally and internationally known speakers on the topic. For example, the speakers included Dr. Franklin H. Littell, Judge Anna Jiagge from Ghana, Dr. Robert Bellah, Dr. John Howard Yoder and Dr. Elise Boulding, sociologist from Dartmouth. An exciting finale for the series was a performance of Peter Ustinov's play, "The Unknown Soldier and his Wife," produced by Council dramatist Paul Sanford.

Later in 1977, Charles Meconis became director of SERPAC, and the threat of militarization became a focus of the committee. Charles

Meconis was a former Roman Catholic priest with a Ph.D. in social ethics from Union Theological Seminary in New York. He was a close friend of the Berrigen brothers, antiwar activists during the Vietnam war. In April 1978 at the request of local denominational leaders, SERPAC held a disarmament conference at St. Mark's Episcopal Cathedral. Speakers were such peace leaders as John Swomley and Marion Anderson. Panels discussed reduction of the threat of nuclear war existing between the Soviet Union and the United States. The conference condemned the proposed placement of Trident submarines at Bangor, a military base on the Kitsap Peninsula. These were considered first strike weapons—one submarine could destroy every major city in the Soviet Union.

Nuclear Disarmament—In retrospect, this conference marked the moment when churches began to coalesce around the issues of nuclear disarmament. Local denominational leaders made this topic the thrust of their annual retreat in May, 1980. In his address to the group, Charles Meconis revealed that he was refusing to pay a portion of his federal income tax because it was a tax to wage war. Archbishop Raymond Hunthausen of the Archdiocese of Seattle, a leader committed to peace, was impressed with Meconis's action and discussed it further with him after the meeting. Ten days later Hunthausen was scheduled to give a speech on peace at the annual meeting of the Lutheran Church of America Pacific Northwest Synod. In his speech the Archbishop called the Bangor Submarine Base "the Auschwitz of Puget Sound" and suggested at the very end of his speech that it would be wonderful if fifty thousand Christian people in the Pacific Northwest would decide to withhold half of their federal income tax and give the money to peace causes. A year later Hunthausen became a war tax resister himself, withholding fifty percent of his federal income tax to protest the nuclear arms race.

Other denominational leaders were supportive of Hunthausen, joining in a special year-long peace protest of the Trident installation. The focus of the ecumenical peace protest was the coming of the USS Ohio in August of 1982.

Silent vigils were held at the gate of the Bangor base throughout the winter, spring and into the summer, working with James and Shelley Douglas in the Ground Zero anti-war group which was located there. When summer came, the bishops and denominational executives announced that they would be on the waters of Hood Canal protesting the coming of the USS Ohio, along with a fleet of small boats that were planning a blockade of the canal. In the fleet of small boats was Jonathan Nelson, the Lutheran Campus Chaplain at the University of Washington and a member of SERPAC, the most outstanding church peace leader in the Seattle area. He had trespassed at the Trident Base many times and had been jailed for it. His small ten foot boat was named the SS Plowshares. In Nelson's boat, along with Charles Meconis and Kim Wahl, was his 78-year-old mother, the late Ruth Youngdahl Nelson, the 1973 American Mother of the Year. She was quoted in *The Source*, the Church Council's newspaper, as saying, "The threat to the world is so vast with the Trident submarine and impending nuclear war that I must take action with my son." At this time also Jonathan Nelson said about his past deeds and what he was about to do, "I am doing alone what I would like to see the Church do corporately, identifying with an act of resistance against evil and thus affirming Christ's love and power." Theirs was a deeply felt Christian witness.

In order to stifle the protest, the U.S. Coast Guard ruled that Hood Canal was off limits and no boats would be allowed on the waters of Hood Canal. This, in effect, would deny and destroy the blockade by the small boats and the denominational leaders' commitment to be on the waters in a silent vigil when the USS Ohio arrived. The Church Council appealed this decision to federal Judge Barbara Rothstein's court and won some limited, but inadequate space on the Canal. The bishops' action finally took place on the more dangerous waters of Puget Sound. The USS Ohio came in early in the morning, unannounced, and under a curtain of darkness. Fortunately, the bishops had made their public witness on the water the day before. The small boat blockade could do little. This was the highest point of visibility by the churches, functioning together, making a strong religious witness for peace. Hunthausen's strong witness and this action by church leaders set the tone and created the space that made possible Target Seattle and other later peace activities in the Seattle area. This entire peace effort had been facilitated and undergirded by the work of SERPAC.

War Tax Resistance—William and Janice Cate joined with Raymond Hunthausen and Charles Meconis in war tax resistance and were later arrested for trespassing at the Trident Base. The Board of Directors of the Church Council was called upon to take a position relative to war tax resistance when an IRS agent came to the Council office and demanded that a tax lien be placed on Charles Meconis's salary. The President-Director told the agent that the Church Council had no policy on this, and he would have to wait until they discussed it. When the Board debated the issue they came to the decision that the government should not put the Church in the position of being the tax collector for the State when it goes against the conscience of a Christian person. They refused to place the lien on Meconis's salary. The Council was no longer harassed by the agent. This policy was also followed when the Cates became war tax resisters.

In the late 1980s, the U.S. Roman Catholic Bishops issued a pastoral letter on peace, and the Church Council of Greater Seattle orchestrated an ecumenical study of the letter by all the denominations. John Boonstra, a United Church of Christ clergyperson who was later to become Executive Director of the Washington Association of Churches, was hired to implement this church-wide study. Seattle, known for being home base for the hawkish Senator Henry Jackson and a place dominated by the military and military thinking was being transformed into a place where there was a strong and vocal peace movement, and the churches were at the center of this energetic witness.

Apartheid in South Africa

The oppressive and unjust system of apartheid in South Africa was gaining the attention of human rights organizations around the world in the late 1970s. Pat Taran, member of the University Friends Meeting and previously mentioned as a human rights activist, brought a proposal to SERPAC and was in turn put on the agenda of the Board of the Church Council. The proposal was in the form of a resolution asking Seattle area banks and lending institutions to refrain from making loans to South Africa as long as apartheid continued. If lending institutions did not comply within a reasonable time, the Church Council would encourage denominations, congregations and individual church members to withdraw their money from these institutions. One member of the Board, a top executive in one of Seattle's largest banks, objected strenuously to the resolution. After heated discussion and debate at its meeting of June 12, 1979, the Board of Directors voted overwhelmingly to approve the resolution, and a South Africa Task Force was formed.

Ms. Tyna Fields, a professor at Shoreline Community College and layperson at the First African Episcopal Methodist Church, was the first chairperson of the new task force. Banks making loans to South Africa were threatened with boycotts if they did not discontinue the practice. There were two banking institutions, Seattle First and Rainier Bank, that had loans with South Africa. Negotiations with CEO's and officers of these banks continued over several years. The bank officers were concerned, but reluctant to make any written statements. Finally, in December, 1985, Seattle First National Bank issued a document stating that the bank would make no more loans, had no more loans or investments in South Africa, and would not sell Krugerrands from South Africa. Soon after this, several black women from the South Africa Council of Churches visited Seattle, and were hosted at a luncheon by executives of Seattle First. One of the South Africa women spoke about the need for divestment of stock in corporations and money in banks doing business in South Africa.

Demonstrations and Arrests—Another focus of the South Africa Task Force was that country's consulate in Seattle. Joseph Swing, the honorary consul, had an office downtown, but when it became the site for weekly demonstrations against apartheid, he closed it and began working out of his home. The weekly demonstrations, held every Sunday afternoon, then moved to his home. A few people would go up to Swing's door, ring the bell and ask to talk to the consul. This was considered trespassing and the city police would arrest them. Many people from the churches and the community, black and white, were arrested week after week. William Cate's story of his arrest gives the feeling of the time:

> Each Sunday three or four people went up the narrow steps to the front door and rang the bell, asking to talk to the Consul. This was considered trespassing and the city police would arrest them. During Christmas week, 1984, Jan, my wife, and our daughter Rebecca attended the rally before the consul's home with Mary Amu El Tayeb, part-time South Africa Task Force staff, and her daughter. The four women went up the steps. Jan and Mary Amu

rang the bell and were arrested. Their pictures were in newspapers and on television. It made South Africa apartheid news in Seattle.

This was during the time I was seriously ill and was limiting my activity. I felt that Jan had made the necessary witness for the whole family. About two weeks later I received a call from Gerald Lenoir of the American Friends Service Committee who was programming the weekly demonstrations. The call came Saturday night after I was in bed and asleep. He asked me to be at the Sunday demonstration next day and be arrested. It was important, he said, because the other three people were African-Americans, and they needed a Caucasian person. Out of the stupor of my sleep I agreed to be there or get someone in my place. In my drowsiness I thought I might ask my associate, David Bloom to be arrested in my place.

When I woke the following morning after a troubled sleep and not feeling well, I realized I could not ask someone to be arrested in my place. Rebecca drove me to the Consul's home. I was very weak. When the time came to trespass, I looked at those mossy, slippery stairs up to the door of the house and wondered if I could make it without falling. My illness had made my legs unsteady. With the three African-American people I made it to the door and rang the bell. Two police officers arrested us, handcuffing our hands behind our back and expecting us to walk down the steep, slippery stairs without using our hands.

I walked slowly down the stairs, expecting to fall any minute. Just before I reached the bottom, an elderly white-haired woman I did not know and have not seen since, stepped out of the crowd at the foot of the stairs, kissed me on the cheek, and helped me to the police car. She was the closest thing to an angel I have experienced. As was its custom, the police car simply went around the block out of sight and released us. We eventually had to appear in court where the judge threw out our case.

When Mary Amu El Tayeb discovered that the Yakima-based Tree Top Apple Juice Company was purchasing South African apple concentrate, the South African Task Force protested. The company quickly divested the product. In the late 1980s Robert Schmidt followed Dr. Fields as chair of the South African Task Force. A trip to

South Africa was planned for several Task Force members. As they waited to leave at Sea-Tac Airport, their visas were denied. Marjorie Prince followed Robert Schmidt as chairperson of the Task Force. Under her leadership, the Task Force began to apply pressure on the local churches to divest themselves of stock they might have in companies doing business in South Africa. An honor roll was established for those churches who did. Marjorie was forced to picket Plymouth Congregational Church, the church to which she belonged.

Urban Ministry

From its beginning, the Church Council of Greater Seattle was an urban ministry dealing with problems of an urban environment. Through the early history of the Council the urban agenda of racial discrimination in schools, unemployment, housing, mental illness and the like, took prominence. There were also issues of Christian unity and interfaith relationships, concerns about peace and human rights around the world as well as a whole range of pastoral care concerns.

It was in the aftermath of the redlining effort in the seventies that a special urban focus began in what was initially called matters of housing and urban decay. David Bloom, an American Baptist minister, was the first chair of the new Urban Development Task Force in 1977, while serving as associate minister of University Baptist Church. In 1978, David joined the Church Council staff as the first program director for the Task Force. At the same time, Steve Bauck, a United Church of Christ minister, became Task Force chair. Later, in 1981, David was elevated to the Church Council's newly created position of Urban Minister.

David felt called to this ministry and had the training and experience to undertake it. He began his work as urban minister in a largely faith operation supported by Wayne Roberts, the executive minister of the American Baptist Churches of the Northwest. Wayne Roberts had these prophetic words to say about David: "He knows the way to City Hall." David Bloom then became the Church Council's Associate Director of Urban Ministry.

When David Bloom began his work in 1978, Seattle City Hall and downtown Seattle soon became aware that the *status quo* was going to be challenged and unexpected, new relationships were going to develop. This was especially so when David began to work closely with

John Fox, a community organizer, on the displacement of low-income renters in downtown Seattle. Many of the older and poorer people lived downtown in small, old hotels. The land value and location of this plethora of old hotels, which provided inexpensive housing for the old and the poor on limited pensions and social security, was prize property and was being gobbled up by developers. These developers had at their disposal subsidized loans and incentives from the federal government which allowed them to build high rise office buildings and luxury hotels. The poor, ill and single working class people were being forced out on to the streets, their housing destroyed without replacement. This was the primary source of the homeless blight that began to plague the city of Seattle in late 1979 and the early 1980s.

Through the cooperative efforts of John Fox and David Bloom, the Seattle Displacement Coalition, an organization of downtown displaced people, was formed. This group was backed by the Urban Development Task Force and the entire Church Council. It organized the primary opposition to the careless disregard for the welfare of the poor on the part of downtown Seattle developers. It was John Fox and David Bloom's opposition to the devastating effect of the developer's plans in displacing people that caused the wrath of the developers to descend on them.

Nonetheless, through the combined efforts of the Church Council, the Seattle Displacement Coalition, the Seattle Tenants Union and other groups, important legislation was passed by the City of Seattle in the late 1970s and early 1980s to protect tenants from displacement. These included a condominium conversion moratorium that led to an ordinance regulating such conversions, a demolition control ordinance, a just-cause eviction ordinance, a rental housing minimum maintenance ordinance, and an ordinance preventing rental housing discrimination based on age or parental status.

Homelessness—Charles Royer, mayor of Seattle, was the featured speaker at the Urban Development Task Force first annual housing conference at St. Mark's Cathedral in April, 1979. It was here that the plight of homeless people was first explored. As a result, the Urban Development Task Force, now called the Task Force on Housing and Homelessness, played a catalytic role among several downtown agencies in establishing the Downtown Emergency Service Center in the old Morrison Hotel to serve the homeless. The Board of Directors of the Council on September 11, 1979 voted to support the venture and appointed the Shelter's initial governing board. The DESC opened on November 19, 1979. During the cold season every night the center would be packed with over two hundred and fifty people of whom approximately one third were mentally ill. Although most of the homeless people were men, there were also many women and some families. This program is still in existence in 1996 as one of the leading multi-service programs serving homeless people in the Northwest.

It was also at this time of the first annual housing conference that the need for more low cost housing was discussed. Steve Claggett, lawyer and Task Force member, suggested that the Urban Development Task Force work jointly with Metro YMCA to form an organization that would provide non-profit technical assistance to churches and community groups who wanted to provide housing for low income people. The program was called Common Ground. Over its fifteen-year history, Common Ground has assisted the development of over fifteen hundred units of low income housing primarily sponsored by churches and other non-profit groups. Common Ground was incorporated separately by the Church Council and the Greater Seattle YMCA shortly after its inception but maintained a close relationship with the Church Council over the years, functioning effectively as a housing development arm of the Council's ministry.

One of the most emotional issues that the Urban Development Task Force brought to the Church Council's regular monthly Board meetings for discussion and decision was an initiative from the Seattle Tenants Union. It was called the Roof Initiative and would impose rent controls on the city's rental housing. The Urban Development Task Force urged the Council to support the passage of the initiative because it would enhance their concern for fair cost housing for low income people. When the Church Council Board of Directors debated the issue at an open meeting there were at least fifty people present from the general community, in addition to the Board itself. Many real estate people from the member churches of the Council were present hoping that the Church Council would reject support of the initiative. The Board voted to support ROOF, but in the public election which followed, the citizens defeated it. It was, however, a compelling example of a forum role the Church Council played in the life of the churches and the general community.

At the annual meeting of the Church Council in May, 1980, housing was the most frequently identified concern. This was the beginning of a preoccupation with housing and homelessness by the Church Council which has lasted over fifteen years. This mandate to work with the homeless was carried out in the later 1980s by a Homeless Task Force with its own staff.

Proposed construction of a convention center over the I-5 corridor in downtown Seattle, oddly enough, became a later housing concern for the Church Council. The Urban Development Task Force urged the Board to oppose this construction because it would further decrease the number of low-cost housing units in Seattle. The freeway corridor had, up to this time, been a "boundary" for commercial building. It was felt that the convention center would provide a bridge, causing developers to be interested in land east of the freeway also. The Church Council publicly opposed this location for a convention center, angering the Downtown Seattle Association. The center was built at that location, and many low cost housing units nearby have been replaced with upscale condominiums. Poor people were displaced once again.

"Filling the Gap"—Cuts to federal social programs, which had been threatened during the Nixon years (1968-1974), became harsh reality after the 1980 election of Ronald Reagan. The mood of the country was conservative. There was little sympathy for people who depended on the government for help. Reagan kept his campaign promises to increase defense spending and cut social welfare. The "truly needy" would be cared for, the new administration said, but in reality more and more people were falling through the cracks.

Churches, of course, were called upon to help where needed. Although the Church Council and its Urban Development Task Force were actively opposing the elimination of social programs, they quickly organized to alleviate suffering in the community brought on by budget cuts. Victor Langford, a Lutheran pastor, directed an effort called "Filling the Gap," which mobilized churches throughout the Seattle area to provide at least some of the human services necessary at this time.

State mental hospitals had been closed, or their operation greatly reduced, during the 1970s. Effective drug treatment for mental disorders made it possible, theoretically, for many people formerly confined to institutions to live productive lives in the community. This was undoubtedly true for some people, but others ended up homeless on the streets of Seattle. The Urban Development Task Force worked creatively with the City of Seattle on one project to ease this crisis. The city purchased and renovated the El Rey Hotel and the Church Council organized churches throughout the area to furnish rooms in the hotel. Sixty rooms were furnished, providing pleasant home surroundings for people formerly living on the streets.

Workers' Rights—In January, 1986, Marc Earls, of the Service Employee International Union AFL-CIO representing local janitors, came to the Council via the Urban Ministry asking for support in their struggle with the owners of the large downtown office buildings. Their complaint was that the building owners and janitorial companies were attempting to cut the already low pay and benefits of the fifteen hundred Local Six members, while increasing workloads. The majority of the union members were women and recent immigrants who spoke very little English. Large and powerful companies were asking these powerless people, receiving marginal salaries at best, to take a cut in their pay that would drop them below the poverty level. The Board of Directors of the Church Council reasoned that the workers would be forced to go to food banks which the Church created or supported subsidizing the welfare of the worker. In effect, the building owners placed upon the churches and the general community the responsibility to support their workers because they were unwilling to pay them a living wage. The Church Council voted to support the union members.

A dramatic interfaith prayer service, coordinated by the Urban Ministry, was held to support the janitors at noon one day in the atrium of the Rainier Tower office building while thousands of office workers were on their lunch hour. The gathering of Christian and Jewish clergy, janitorial workers and their supporters provided an enormous boost for the workers. This, plus the publicity of church support, personal letters from clergy to building owners, and clergy meetings with building owners contributed significantly to a satisfactory settlement for the janitors. The president of the service employees union described the effectiveness of the religious community's support as follows: "The religious community was an essential element of our success. By defining the building owners' efforts to impoverish local janitors as a moral issue, and one of concern to the community as a whole, Seattle's religious community sent the building owners a message that their efforts were an attack on the community as a whole and its moral standards."

On October 13, 1987, a similar request to the Church Council came through the Urban Ministry from Swedish Hospital workers, again composed mainly of women and new immigrants, who were threatening to strike. On the basis of its previous decision the Council voted to support the union. Over the years the Church Council had hesitated to enter into labor-management issues because of the possibility of harming the collective bargaining process. In the situations mentioned it was the issue of greater power versus powerless and marginal people.

The State of the City Report was another creative idea issuing from the Urban Ministry. This annual report was delivered in the spring of each year starting in 1984, after the Mayor's State of the City Report and before the Church Council annual meeting. The report analyzed the condition of the city within a theological and ethical context. Each year a different aspect of human need was analyzed and brought to the attention of the people and the city's political leaders.

In 1988, the Council's Urban Ministry started a new housing program called the Homelessness Project. This new housing effort was supported through a major, multi-year grant from the Department of Housing and Urban Development. It was set up to recruit local churches to provide long-term transitional housing (six months to two years) for homeless women with children. Project staff screen qualified families, provide case management and assist the families in receiving the support and training they need to become self-sufficient, enabling them to live on their own. By 1995, ten churches were involved and fifty families had been assisted.

Areas of Pastoral Concern

Issues of Aging—One of the harsh realities of urban life is that large numbers of people are away from extended family and must deal with the problems and decisions of aging alone. This area of concern came to the attention of the Church Council as a pastoral need in the Seattle area, and the Task Force on Aging was formed. In 1984, Mary Liz Chaffee offered to serve as part-time staff for this task force. She could and did give strong leadership to the program, as she was a nurse with the Catholic Community Services Chore Ministry, a program working with aging and disabled people in their homes. Mary Liz Chaffee brought together church and community workers with the aging to discuss and confront a whole range of problems facing aging people. The Task Force was able to perform an exceptional collaborative service among a variety of groups in church and community concerned with aging problems. It served as a resource to people in the churches and community dealing with family members who needed assistance. For many years the Task Force cooperated with Catholic Community Services in spreading the Chore Ministry program to many of the Protestant churches. Although based in a Catholic social agency, the Chore Ministry operated in a truly ecumenical fashion, thanks to the Task Force on Aging.

Issues of People with Handicapping Conditions—Another task force that had a short but important life was the Church Council's Handicapped Task Force. Its one illustrious event was the celebration of the International Year of the Disabled at Hec Edmunson Pavilion at the University of Washington. This was designed to raise the awareness of the church and community about issues related to being handicapped in modern urban society. The service of worship with music was conducted by people with handicapping conditions. The preacher for the event was a nationally known United Church of Christ clergyperson, Harold Wilke, who was born with no arms but can function normally in the pulpit and in all of life. The service was designed to be handicap accessible, and was attended by hundreds of disabled people with their families and friends. This event raised the consciousness of churches in the area about the need for church buildings to be accessible to everyone.

Issues of Mental Health—It was mentioned earlier that the Urban Development Task Force had advocated and helped to provide housing for mentally ill people. The Church Council had recognized for some time the need for pastoral care for people with mental illness, and in 1987 was able to fill that need when Craig Rennebohm, a United Church of Christ clergyperson, became mental health chaplain. He has been able to work with mentally ill people on the streets.

Craig has worked with churches throughout the area and has trained many others to work in mental health ministry.

Family Life Issues—Long before the new religous right "rediscovered" it, the Council had undertaken a ministry to strengthen the family. The Church Council's Family Life Task Force began under the leadership of a Lutheran pastor, Charles May, in the late 1970s with the initial effort simply to define what is meant by family. This led to an investigation of this basic unit of all human existence, and the awareness grew that the modern nuclear family was both a problem and a myth. In the last few years of the Task Force's life, leadership was given by Rosemary Christlaw who helped to uncover the many resources that are available to strengthen family life through the Church.

Focus on World Issues in the 1980s

It was stated earlier that President Jimmy Carter attempted to focus attention on human rights around the world but that the mood of the country was to focus more on cold war and domestic issues. However, the Church could not ignore what was happening to people wherever they were. A discussion follows about several instances of Council action in the area of human rights.

Central America—In the late 1970s the Seattle area began to have large numbers of Central American refugees who had come across the Mexican border illegally to escape military dictatorships in Nicaragua, Guatemala and El Salvador. How were the churches going to relate to these persecuted and illegal aliens? The United States government had supported the oppressive regimes in these countries and now wanted to return the refugees home because their presence here was embarrassing. The government's policy toward the refugees was carried out with a vengeance by the Immigration Naturalization Service. The Church Council Board of Directors passed resolutions during this time urging the United States government:

1. To cease all military and economic aid to the Somoza regime in Nicaragua;

2. Not to intervene on behalf of the military powers in El Salvador;

3. To give sanctuary to people from these countries as political refugees.

The Council established a Central American Task Force in 1981, and one of the first issues addressed was whether or not churches should provide sanctuary for Central American refugees. They studied the issue and sought agreement from the Council Board and among denominational leaders. An interdenominational worship service at St. James Cathedral in November, 1992, provided the setting for the Church Council's call to churches to provide sanctuary for Central American refugees.

Several churches responded to the call. University Baptist Church responded with enthusiasm, and subsequently its pastor, Donovan Cook, played a major role in giving focus to the effort of religious groups in the area to oppose United States support of military governments in Central America. The Seattle City Council passed a resolution declaring Seattle a sanctuary city, and Managua, Nicaragua became our sister city. William Cate joined the mayor, Jewish rabbis, and Archbishop Raymond Hunthausen in welcoming several groups of Central American refugees to sanctuary in the churches and synagogues around the city.

Due primarily to the leadership of El Centro De la Raza, a Seattle Hispanic center, many Seattle area people, including a great number from churches, visited Nicaragua and El Salvador in the 1980s. Celebration of the martyrdom of Oscar Romero, Archbishop of El Salvador and the suffering people of El Salvador and Central America became the source of an annual religious procession between Roman Catholic and Protestant churches with a prayer service that followed. It usually took place the third Sunday afternoon in March, in Seattle. The Church Council was one of the prime sponsors of this new ecumenical worship tradition.

In the midst of this torrent of religious activity centered around Central America, the Seattle area churches became aware of liberation theology and the special option the Christian Gospel has for the poor and oppressed of the world. They became aware how far the Christian people of Seattle, as well as the general population of Seattle, had moved in their understanding of the nation's role in Central America. The political leaders were supporting military regimes and dictators. The Church Council, on the other hand, gave leadership in throwing the influence of the Church in Seattle behind the welfare of the poor and oppressed. Therefore, the Council opposed the U.S. government's support of the Contras who were seeking to destabilize the Sandinista government in Nicaragua and urged no support to the military government of El Salvador. The churches discovered that they had a concept of foreign policy for Central America that was different from that held by the White House and Congress.

Japanese-American Redress—An issue that goes back to the Second World War reappeared, seeking resolution. When Japanese-American people of the Seattle area were relocated to resettlement concentration camps away from the west coast at the beginning of World War II, the old Seattle Council of Churches was one of the very few groups that objected. In 1971 a caucus of Asian pastors had addressed the Board of Directors of the Council telling of their special concerns. One of the most important issues was the need for redress to Japanese-American people who were imprisoned for over four years during the war and as a result, lost all of their possessions. When a Japanese-American woman presented the need for redress to the Council she broke into tears, saying, "It is difficult for me to talk about the issue, and it has been impossible for my parents." The silence was finally broken and the Church Council threw its influence behind the effort for redress. It came almost too late for many of the people who were harmed because many were already dead.

The Domingo-Viernes Case—Another incident that affected Asian people and tested the Church Council's commitment to human rights was the Domingo-Viernes case. Two Filipino-American Cannery Union leaders, Selme Domingo and Gene Viernes, were assassinated in 1981, and their killers were apprehended immediately. It was believed by the families, however, that the assassins had been hired by President Ferdinand Marcos of the the Philippines because Domingo and Viernes had been strongly anti-Marcos. The actual killers were locally hired hit men.

The Domingo family, wanting to bring Marcos and the killers to justice, came to the Church Council for support. The Council voted to support them in any way that they could. It provided a non-profit base. William Cate and Timothy Nakayama kept in close contact with

Selme's sister, Cynthia Domingo, who gave strong leadership to the lengthy law suit. During this period Cindy also served on the Executive Committee and the Board of Directors of the Council.

The killers were quickly convicted of their crime, but to prove the complicity of Marcos was another thing, since the assassination was international in scope. It seemed impossible. But Cindy and the legal team persisted. It all ended December 8, 1989, eight years after the assassination, when in Judge Barbara Rothstein's federal court, the Domingo and Viernes families won a civil conviction against the now dead Ferdinand and his wife Imelda with a 15.1 million dollar judgment against their estate. During the latter part of this period the Church Council stayed in close touch with the fall of the dictatorship of Marcos in the Philippines through the Asia Pacific Task Force of the Council.

Timothy Nakayama and Cindy Domingo also served as co-chairs of the task force which focused on the Pacific Islands and Asia.

A Church Council Foreign Policy—In terms of a foreign policy based on a Christian value system, Robert Schmidt, a Missouri Synod Lutheran chaplain at the University of Washington, accomplished an amazing feat. Schmidt had just completed his work for a doctorate in political science at the University of Washington. He presented a plan to the Council which required the total involvement of all the various task forces that were focused on world political and human rights problems. Scholars were recruited to write papers on special areas such as the Soviet Union, Korea, the Philippines, Israel, South Africa and so on. All papers were predicated on a value structure which reflected the Christian ethic. Public hearings were held three Tuesdays in January, 1984, at St. Mark's Cathedral. A full crowd attended the hearings, and several of the articles were eventually printed in the daily press or in *The Source*.

Schmidt then suggested the impossible. He asked that the Board of Directors vote on policy statements in these areas of political concern. This was done at an extended Board meeting chaired by Peter Raible, minister of the University Unitarian Church. The Council now had an official foreign policy. A few people felt it was done hurriedly, but all felt it was an amazing feat.

Israel and Jewish-Christian Issues—Another related human rights issue affected the Church Council's ability to carry out its ecumenical task in the Seattle area. In February, 1981, William Cate and four other Seattle clergy (Rodney Romney, Pastor of First Baptist Church in Seattle, Melvin Finkbeiner, Pastor of University United Methodist Temple, Casper Glenn, Presbyterian Synod Executive, and Richard Washington, Episcopal Campus Chaplain) accepted an invitation from Farhat Ziedeh to visit the Palestinian people and the Palestinian Liberation Organization (PLO) in Beirut, Lebanon. KING Television news staff and Priscilla Collins, chairperson of KING's Board of Directors, accompanied the group. Jewish leaders in Seattle were very critical of Cate's participation in the visit. Cate, on returning, claimed that the PLO was a legitimate representative of the Palestinian people; Yasser Arafat, head of the PLO, was a moderate; and the Palestinian people needed a homeland.

A crisis in Jewish-Christian relations in the Council ensued. There had been Jewish observers on the Board of Directors of the Council from its very early days. This relationship had led to the creation of a dialogue and study group of Christian clergy and Jewish rabbis that had met monthly year after year. This new crisis was a challenge for the Council in keeping up communication with the Jewish leaders. The long standing monthly study group of Jewish and Christian clergy was very important in maintaining open communication. It is still continuing stronger than ever.

Programs followed that helped the Jewish community to realize that support of the rights of Palestinians did not mean the Council was not supportive of Israel's needs and Jewish concerns. The Church Council joined with Jewish groups and others in April, 1983, at Seattle University in presenting a conference on the Holocaust. It was co-chaired by Elaine Stanovsky and Sidney Stock. The Jewish community was still not satisfied with relationships with the Council over Near East issues.

In September 1987, Ira Stone, a Conservative Jewish rabbi, presented the idea of a Christian-Jewish Task Force of the Church Council that would expedite communication between the Church Council and the Jewish leaders. This was done and Barbara Hurst, director of the Seattle branch of the American Jewish Committee, was elected as chairperson. Relationships improved and the Task Force sponsored such activities as a traveling exhibit from Holland in the fall of 1988 on the life and times of Anne Frank, the young Jewish girl who was killed by the Nazis during the Holocaust.

Church State Issues

The Church Council issued a policy statement which guided them through the 1970s and 1980s regarding the separation of Church and State, particularly as this related to public schools. The policy statement said, in part, "Above all we have been guided by our own sense of what is necessary for education in a pluralistic society. For us that means no religious practice in institutions of public education. For us that means freedom from molestation because of religious belief or lack of religious belief. For us that means freedom to express one's belief in ways that do not molest or harass others." This statement served the Council well for many years and went unchallenged until the late 1980s, when it was questioned by the Religious Right.

A Time for Dialogue

A continuing area of concern was the split that exists in Protestantism between the mainline Protestants and the Evangelical and the Fundamentalist Protestants. The definition of just who belongs in each of these groups is not very clear. It is clear, however, that few of the Evangelical churches were members of the Council and none of the Fundamentalists were. The new political involvement of the Religious Right accentuated the need for new dialogue among the groups. Some of the Evangelical groups participated in Friend to Friend, the Emergency Feeding Program and in the Youth Center Chaplaincy Program. Frank Spina, professor of religion at Seattle Pacific University and a Free Methodist clergyman, was chair for several years of the Christian Century Lectureship and led Bible study in many of the mainline Protestant churches.

At the fall assembly of the Church Council in 1982 Spina and Tom Sine, an Evangelical social activist, spoke on the topic, "Evangelicalism, Social Justice and the Church." It was generally concluded from the presentation that the differences that separate Evangelicals and mainline Protestants have little to do with theology, but more to do with culture, economics and history. The session eased tension between the groups in the Seattle area. There have been no public dis-putes among the groups. Cooperation between them, however, is still minimal.

New Interfaith Developments—In the 1980s, unexpectedly, the Church of Jesus Christ Latter Day Saints (Mormons) applied to be an Interfaith Partner on the Board of Directors of the Church Council of Greater Seattle. This represented a moving out by them from their former isolation. One of the most rapidly growing religious groups in the area, they were interested in hunger issues. They had a repre-sentative for some time on the governing board of the Emergency Feeding Program. Representation was later sought by them on the newly created Interfaith Council of Washington. By this time, with the addition of the Chinook Learning Center, there were six religious groups who had representation on the Church Council Board as In-terfaith Partners. For the time being it served as a vehicle of interfaith cooperation on selected community issues.

IX

Completing a Busy Decade, 1985-1990

William B. Cate

EIGHT hundred people gathered on October 11, 1984, at the Seattle Center Exhibition Hall to help the Church Council of Greater Seattle celebrate its fifteenth birthday. Emory Bundy, Truxton Ringe, and Jessie Kinnear Kenton planned and executed the party. The Rev. Cecil Williams, Pastor of Glide Memorial United Methodist Church in San Francisco, was the speaker of the evening. William Cate, though ill and recuperating in the hospital, agreed to serve a fourth and final five-year term as President-Director. A reflective look at the first fifteen years of the Council was indeed revealing:

> The budget had grown from $69,000 in 1970 to $1,939,699 in 1984.
> The Council was no longer borrowing from next year's money to pay current year expenses.
> The Church Council newspaper's role in interpreting the work of the Church Council to the churches had begun to pay dividends to the institutional well-being of the Council.
> Task forces which had been established who had done their work now no longer existed.

Some programs, such as SERPAC, Native American Task
Force, Friend to Friend, Emergency Feeding Program,
Task Force on Aging, Youth Center Chaplaincy continued.
The operation had grown enough to need more core staff.
Alice Woldt was hired as Associate Director of Administra-
tion. David Bloom became the Associate Director of Urban
Ministry.
The President-Director, or one of the Associate Directors,
could provide staff representation to each task force,
improving communication between staff and program.
The Council had made its point that the Church in the
Seattle area was in fact one Church and could act effec-
tively on peace and justices issues as one body when circumstances demanded it.

Thus began William Cate's final term as President-Director, and
the Council continued to work tirelessly for peace and justice in the
community and in the world.

Christian Century Lectureship

This program was developed by the Council in cooperation with
the Christian Century Journal and Foundation to bring speakers to
the area in an effort to raise awareness about important peace and
justice issues. Martin Marty, Lutheran historian and writer; James
Cone, African-American theologian; and Rosalyn Carter, former first
lady, were among the outstanding speakers featured.

Leningrad-Seattle Sister Churches Program

In the late 1980s cracks were developing in the "iron curtain," and
the Church in the Soviet Union was indicating a desire to communi-
cate with churches in the West. Paul Riley and Peter Anderson, Roman Catholic lay people, were instrumental in getting the Leningrad-
Seattle Sister Churches Task Force started at the Church Council.
The Task Force sent a delegation to Leningrad and asked what help
could be given. The Leningrad churches suggested that we could help
by sending Bibles in the Russian language. TheTask Force set a goal
to raise money for ten thousand Bibles. In December, 1989, Lutheran
Bishop Lowell Knutson traveled to Leningrad to present ten thousand Bibles to church leaders there. Earlier that year, Russian Ortho-

dox Metropolitan Aleksiy led a delegation to Seattle to learn how a church functions in a free society. They were particularly interested in religious education and in jail and hospital chaplaincy programs. The delegation from Leningrad (now St. Petersburg) represented Lutheran, Roman Catholic, Seventh Day Adventist and Russian Orthodox churches. A public celebration was held for them at the Church Council's fall assembly on September 18, 1989, at the University Presbyterian Church.

The relationship between the churches of St. Petersburg and Seattle continued to grow after the fall of communisn in Russia. The administration of Providence Hospital of Seattle offered resources to help with the operation of a small hospital in St. Petersburg. In June of 1990 Metropolitan Aleksiy was elevated to be the Patriarch of the Russian Orthodox Church of all of Russia.

The Bishops' Apology to Native Americans

The Native American Task Force of the Church Council had labored long to support the treaty rights of the Native American people in the Pacific Northwest, and a high degree of trust had developed between the Task Force and Indian people. In March of 1987, Jewel Praying Wolf James, one of the spiritual leaders of the Lummi Indian Tribe, asked the Church Council to request church leaders of the state of Washington to apologize formally for their role in past efforts to eliminate Native American religion. Religious and political leaders through the years had participated in the systematic destruction of Native American culture and religion. William Cate took this request to the denominational leaders' annual planning meeting, and they agreed to act. For several months they worked under the leadership of the chairperson of the Native American Task Force, Jon Magnuson, Lutheran Campus Chaplain, who actually wrote the first draft of the Apology in a sacred Native American burial ground in New Mexico. Magnuson said that there he could feel the presence of the spirits of the ancestors. Finally, after much work, the denominational leaders made the Apology their own, apologizing for past deeds and asking forgiveness and the blessing of the native people.

The Apology is a profound and touching document. It was delivered by the Church leaders to the Native American leaders on the Saturday before Thanksgiving, 1987, on the site of an ancient Indian burial ground in downtown Seattle. The site is now covered over by pavement and buildings. Amid the beating of drums, singing and prayers the Apology was presented by Episcopal Bishop Robert Cocherane in behalf of the church leaders to the Native American people. After this event the Apology was read in many of the eighteen hundred congregations in the state of Washington whose denominational leaders had signed the statement. It was also immediately read publicly in all the smokehouses of the twenty-eight tribes of the state of Washington. The Apology later made its way to South America, then around the world to all indigenous peoples.

Madrona Point—In the Apology, church leaders committed themselves to help the Native American people protect their holy places. This commitment was tested almost immediately when Kurt Rousseau, representing the Lummi Tribe, asked churches for help to save an ancient Indian burial ground threatened by the development at Madrona Point on Orcas Island. The developer was a powerful timber executive who wanted to build eighty condominiums on the site. The Task Force agreed to explore how it might help, since negotiations between the Lummis and the developer had broken down. The Task Force, led by Jon Magnuson and Task Force staff Ronald Adams intervened in the situation, but with little success.

Due to this, in cooperation with the Lummis, the Church leaders, led by the Task Force, held simultaneous prayer vigils at Madrona Point and at the downtown headquarters of the development company to dramatize the problem. The media picked up the story. Unexpectedly, William Randolph Hearst III became interested. Through him, James Waldo, a mediator, was secured who brought the parties back to the table. In the end, the development company got a good price for the land. The Lummis preserved their sacred burial ground, and the island people obtained a beautiful 32-acre park on Orcas Island. The Church had the satisfaction of knowing that it had been faithful to its pledge.

The Church Council played a pivotal role in saving the sacred place. It was a classic public expression of economic power in conflict with spiritual power with the latter being victorious. This was not the last time that the Native American Task Force of the Church Council would be asked to help save a sacred place for Native American people. The story of the preservation of Snoqualmie Falls will be told later.

Freedom in Worship—Mention should be made of another Native American concern in which the Task Force became involved. In 1989 the case of Al Smith, a Klamath Indian, versus the State of Oregon came before the United States Supreme Court for review. Smith, working as a social worker in a drug program in the state of Oregon, had been fired when he participated in a Native American Church Service which traditionally uses the hallucinogenic drug, peyote. Because of this, the State of Oregon refused to pay him unemployment compensation. The issue raised was can the state dictate to a religious community which sacraments are considered sacred by the religious group? The national Native American community rallied around Smith and asked the Church Council's support since Christian leaders in our area had pledged to support Indians in preserving religious objects sacred to them. The Task Force sent James Halfaker, a United Church of Christ regional executive, and William Cate to the U.S. Supreme Court hearing in Washington DC and to a Native American Rally that followed it. The Church stood with the Native American people. Unfortunately, the issue has not yet been totally resolved.

One final episode with the Native American community was minor, but was interesting. In 1989 a Wisconsin entrepreneur and anti-Indian racist produced beer for sale in Washington state and called it Treaty Beer. Some of the profit, he said, would be used to fight Indian treaties, thus the name. Local Native American leaders and the Church Council landed on Treaty Beer while the advertising copy was still wet. Newspapers and politicians joined in opposing it as a hate campaign. Treaty Beer never made it in Washington state.

Interfaith Council

As the latter part of the twentieth century approached, Seattle was not just a Christian and Jewish religious community. Buddhist, Hindu, Islamic and other religious communities had become significant voices in the area. The Church Council had a relationship with some through its provision for Interfaith Partners, but that was not enough to facilitate broad scale dialogue.

Peter Raible, pastor of University Unitarian Church, had been concerned about this for some time. There was no single person or party, however, responsible for the formation of the Interfaith Council of Washington in October 1987. In addition to Raible, Rabbi Anson Laytner and Rabbi James Mirel had nurtured the dream. Swami Bhaskarananda of the Vedanta Society (Hindu) and Pasha Mohajer-Jasbi of the Baha'i Faith were also influential in this endeavor. William Cate represented the Christian community. The Interfaith Council saw itself as primarily a dialogue group. It had some union services in which peace, viewed in spiritual terms, was expressed and celebrated by the various groups. Their biggest venture took place on June 1, 1990, when the Interfaith Council sponsored a performance of Beethoven's Ninth Symphony in connection with the Goodwill Games. This was facilitated by a member of the Latter Day Saints community, Dana Davenport.

Some Further Peace Issues

During the late 1980s the Council took numerous stands on peace issues. Among them:

Voted to urge political leaders to ban nuclear testing by our government.

Voted to oppose all funding for "Star Wars."

Protested visit by South Korean President because of his country's dictatorial rule.

Opposed the establishment of a naval base in Everett, Washington.

Washington State Centennial

In preparation for the 100th birthday of the State of Washington in 1989, the Church Council signed in 1987 a contract with two historians, David Buerge and Junius Rochester, to write a history of religion in the state. The first chapter was dedicated to Native American religion. Over four thousand copies of the book, *Roots and Branches*, were sold. Leaders of the Centennial celebration said that this was by far the best of several histories written for the year-long event.

Religion and the Arts

The Church Council of Greater Seattle sought to support religious art in various forms through the years. As mentioned earlier, religious dramas were presented throughout the area, the most popular being *Godspell*. A Worship and Arts festival was sponsored at St. Mark's Cathedral. Patrinell Wright, conductor of the Total Experience Gospel Choir, led the celebration of Martin Luther King's Birthday with music and drama, playing to a packed auditorium. This event was jointly sponsored by the Church Council, Black Clergy for Action, and Seattle First United Methodist Church.

Esther "Little Dove" John established the Task Force on Mission for Music and Healing in the late 1980s. Little Dove, an accomplished flutist, had walked by herself across the United States and Europe to Russia for peace. She combines her dedication to peace and ecology with her love for music in this new ministry. She uses music in the cause of world peace, spiritual growth, alleviation of suffering and loneliness, and in the appreciation of our natural environment. She plays in hospitals, hospices, nursing homes, churches, private homes and concert halls.

Farm Workers

An unlikely area of ministry for the Church Council was with the farm workers, since they were living mostly in rural areas. During the 1970s and 1980s the Council supported boycotts of certain crops in solidarity with Caesar Chavez and the United Farm Worker's Union. Chavez visited Seattle on two occasions to ask for church support in eliminating the use of toxic sprays. Church Women United was especially helpful in supporting the boycotts. The Church Council traditionally viewed farm workers issues as belonging to the Washington Association of Churches. A Farm Workers Support Task Force was, however, made a part of the Church Council, which meant that the Council was expected to join forces with them in their efforts to organize a labor union in the State of Washington. Negotiations were particularly aimed at the Chateau Ste. Michelle Winery in Woodinville, and the boycott of their wines. Though it seemed hopeless at times, the workers at Ste. Michelle were finally permitted to vote in 1995 and now have their union.

Celebrations

Although worship was not a special focus of the Church Council, special worship events have been important vehicles of unity and justice through the years. People have gathered in services of worship for peace, for human rights in Central America and South Africa, in solidarity with Native Americans, and for our environment, lifting our concerns to God and praying for divine guidance. On some occasions, Christians have simply gathered as "one Church" to express thanks for some victory won over ignorance, greed and fear.

Special mention should be made here of David Aasen, pastor of the First United Methodist Church of Seattle, for his ecumenical spirit and generosity in offering his church and himself for countless concerts, plays, lectures, rallies, dinners and programs for the Church Council. He was one of the creators of *Joyspell* , a worship event each January featuring such people over the years as Howard Thurman, Steve Allen, the Total Experience Choir and others.

In Conclusion

Nearly 800 people jammed the Exhibition Hall at the Seattle Center on the evening of May 5, 1990. They were there to honor William Cate for twenty years as President-Director of the Church Council of Greater Seattle, and to wish him well on retirement. It was announced that evening that Elaine Stanovsky, a United Methodist clergyperson, would be Cate's successor.

As William Cate reflected on the twenty years, some questions came to mind:

How well did the Church Council serve as a facilitator of church unity?—It can be affirmed that the Church Council did increase and manifest the unity of the Church. The basic understanding of the oneness of the Church in the community of Greater Seattle undergirded all that the Council did. Sometimes this understanding was not as apparent to the community as it might have been, due to the focus on getting the job done—the job of serving human need and working for justice. Perhaps the "oneness" of the Church is best expressed at such times as when church leaders joined Raymond Hunthausen in the highly visible witness for peace while protesting the approach of the Trident submarine to Bangor Naval Base. And the spirit of the Living God was certainly present in the Bishops' Apology to Native Americans. When the Church Council, in behalf of Christian churches, reached out to take the hands of Interfaith Partners, the God of history must have been pleased.

Did the Church Council really heal any of the brokenness in Greater Seattle?—Programs to serve the poor, the hungry, the homeless, were certainly helpful. Efforts to stand with the oppressed and powerless people against the insensitive powerful were not so clearly successful. The Church Council sought to be faithful to the Gospel, which makes no sense to the powerful and rich. Church Council leaders, such as John Fox and David Bloom, were criticized severely by the Downtown Seattle Association for standing with displaced people on the streets of Seattle. Just as the prophets of old were stoned, these men stood with the victims of human greed and were blamed by those who were powerful. There can be no lasting peace until justice is realized for all people. The Church Council increased justice for marginal people, but never enough.

One of the lessons learned through the twenty year experience of the Church Council is that one cannot be a healer and a reconciler if one is not fully involved in the crisis at hand. The Council learned, often painfully, that reconciliation in a situation of conflict predicated on injustice cannot be obtained until the injustice is rectified.

Looking back over the twenty years, the very distinctive change in the Council's style of operation over against other similar church councils across the nation was the deliberate move from being only a service agency to making the Council an instrument of justice in God's world.

Could more have been accomplished with more money?— The most constant complaint heard was that "we could have done more if we had had more money." It is true there may have been less hardship on the staff if they had had more funds, but money was never the major hindrance. The greatest shortcoming was always lack of vision and commitment.

Many significant people were named in these highlights of the Cate years at the Church Council of Greater Seattle, and many significant people who played key leadership roles were omitted. The great cloud of witnesses that bore up the Council over the years was made up of all those individuals who give sacrificially to support the

Council with their time, their treasure and their dreams. Likewise some crucial programs have been just mentioned and not described. The Vice Presidents who served with William Cate carried heavy responsibility. They are:

John Mitchell	Roman Catholic
Dorothy Hollingsworth	African Methodist Episcopal
Diana Bader	Roman Catholic
Sally Mackey	Presbyterian
Timothy Nakayama	Episcopal
Tyna Fields	African Methodist Episcopal
Mark Hillman	Evangelical Lutheran Church of America
Truxton Ringe	United Church of Christ
Laura Bailey	Christian, Disciples of Christ

X

The One and the Many, 1990-1995

Elaine J. W. Stanovsky

IN ITS FIRST two decades, 1970-90, the newly configured Church Council of Greater Seattle evolved and expanded its scope significantly, reflecting the many changes in the society in which its churches functioned. By1990, the Council had grown into an organization that combined a variety of centers of passion and energy which emerged from the grass roots of the church and community.

Each of these centers of activity, once it received approval from the Board of Directors and the Planning Committee, gathered its own group of supporters and formed its own policy-setting board or task force. And each operated with a remarkable degree of autonomy. The glue that held this all together was William B. Cate, who had been present for the birth of each group and knew its leadership personally.

When Bill Cate announced his plans to retire after twenty years, there was genuine uncertainty whether the diverse emphases within the Council could hold together and survive with new leadership. In preparation for the transition, the Board of Directors initiated an in-depth self-study producing a set of recommendations that informed the search for the new director, and significantly shaped the future initiatives of the Council. The study pointed to the need for greater involvement by member congregations, so that the Council could become more deeply rooted in the life of the Church. In particular, it was hoped that minority churches would participate more fully, and that intergroup relations would be strengthened. Women's concerns still needed to be addressed, and spirituality and worship deserved increased emphasis.

Having laid this groundwork, the Council selected the Rev. Elaine J. W. Stanovsky, a local church pastor, to be its next leader. To signal a renewed emphasis on congregational relations, Stanovsky was introduced to the church community in a series of ten dinners around the greater Seattle area, coordinated by the Rev. David Aasen and June Whitson. This began a new pattern for taking the Church Council out into the churches, a pattern that continues today.

The challenge for the diverse components of the Council during these years was to discover and affirm their shared identity and to develop a true organizational center. The Rev. Paul Flucke (University Congregational United Church of Christ), chair of the powerful Planning Committee of the Church Council, was quoted in the *Seattle Times* in 1990 as describing the Council as a federation of autonomous programs united by a common postage meter. Although this was a deliberate overstatement, it was true that the organization needed to identify and articulate its overall mission.

In a "State of the Council" address in 1991, Stanovsky cited a little-known review of the Council prepared in 1986 by Don Hopps, of the Archdiocese of Seattle. Hopps noted that the decentralized organization of the Council contributed to inefficiencies in operation. He reported that, "The structure more than centers on the President-Director; it is entirely dependent on that position for internal communication, direction and coherence." Further, he found that, "Many actions are taken in the name of the Council that are not owned by it or, more especially, its members."

Programs were often loosely tied to the rest of the Council, governed by autonomous boards or task forces, and their work inadequately interpreted to the church community. This led to congregational alienation, jeopardized local church funding and support for the Council, compromised internal coordination among various programs, and eroded program confidence in the central core of the organization: administrative staff and the Board of Directors.

Organizational Change

During the early 1990s, the organization began the slow process of change. In response to recommendations by the Council's auditor, financial and accounting procedures were systematized and centralized. Following initiatives by the Planning Committee under the new leadership of the Rev. Barbara Wells (Woodinville Unitarian Universalist Association) program review became more rigorous, and greater care was taken in the process of program initiation or adoption to ensure that groups understood and supported the mission and vision of the Church Council. Council leadership came to understand that, though programs paid administrative fees, every program cost more than it contributed, forcing tighter scrutiny of programs asking to come under the Council's umbrella. In addition to administrative changes, several initiatives were undertaken that transformed the Council's self-understanding, and its way of doing business.

Board Operations—Following the 1991 "State of the Council" remarks, Stanovsky appointed a Board Operations Task Group to review how the Board of Directors conducted business. For two years this group reviewed and evaluated the Council, focusing on the role of the Board of Directors. One recommendation led to the first all day Board Retreat in many years in the fall of 1994, which helped the Board appreciate its own diversity, and begin to develop a shared vision for the future. The Board initiated a process of in-depth study and deliberation of controversial issues. Issues brewing on the horizon were presented and discussed a month or two before action was anticipated. Because of this innovation, by the time a proposal for action was presented, the Board was already familiar with the issues at stake. Finally, the work of the Board Operations Task Group encouraged Directors to work intentionally at becoming an ecumenical community of care for one another.

Action Planning—Terryl Ross led the Council in a broad self-study program in 1994. He met with every program and task force and administrative group in the life of the Council, asking about their part in the whole. Then he held a series of consultation sessions, where representatives of various groups met together. Based upon the ideas he heard in these consultations, he proposed several Council-wide projects to help the many programs in the Council live their way into a shared identity. In response to an expressed need for clearer, more consistent internal communication, a newsletter was developed that circulated among staff and volunteers. Also, volunteer needs in local churches and church-sponsored programs were identified, and a Volunteer Village was instituted to link volunteers with opportunities for service. Perhaps most important, through this process of consultation, the constituent parts of the Council became more aware and appreciative of one another, and of the complexity of the organization to which they belonged. Greater cooperation in fund development, in particular, resulted from this new awareness of the whole Council.

Systems Inventory—Following on Terryl's work, Jan Van Pelt led the Council in another self-study. The results showed that, compared to other organizations, the Council was spontaneous and its authority was "discretionary" in the extreme. These characteristics were shown to contribute to a low level of strategic planning, confusion about identity and decision making, a sense of disconnection between programs, and relatively high level of conflict within the organization.

One area where these traits were most visible and troubling was in the area of fund development. Because of the high degree of autonomy and low level of coordination, the various branches of the Church Council family were competing with one another for scarce resources. At times funding agencies received applications from several programs of the Council at the same time, totally uncoordinated. Funding agencies became frustrated and even angry that they were being asked to prioritize programs that the Council itself had not prioritized. The self-interest of the program groups motivated them to work for more coordination and common mission. In a climate of shrinking dollars and higher expectations, programs began working together to articulate a coordinated programmatic mission, and to share information and resources for fund development.

Public Witness

While reweaving the fabric of the organization, the Council continued its prophetic witness in the public arena.

The Gulf War: a Witness for Peace

Iraq invaded Kuwait during the summer of 1990. The Board of Directors had adopted a resolution "Regarding Mid-East Crisis" in August, condemning Iraq's annexation of Kuwait, opposing deployment of U. S. troops to the region and urging non-violent resolution of the conflict.

During the fall, the Peace Task Force, under the leadership of the Rev. Barbara Wells, chair, and Len Schreiner, staff, organized opportunities for public prayer for peace, and clergy gatherings to discuss the threat of war in the region. When the United Nations announced a January 15 deadline for Iraqi withdrawal from Kuwait, the Task Force announced plans for a candlelight peace procession on the night of January 14, the eve of the deadline. The walk began at St. James Cathedral (Roman Catholic) and ended at St. Mark's Cathedral (Episcopal) with prayers by Christian, Jewish and Muslim leaders. It was the largest public witness for peace and against United States military involvement in the conflict in the nation.

By the end of the week the United States had attacked Iraq. Protesters encamped at the Federal Building in downtown Seattle. Tensions rose. Norm Rice, mayor of Seattle, called a meeting of the Seattle police and leaders of peace groups. He began the meeting by recalling that the Seattle City Council was on record opposing this war, and asserting that the police and the protesters shared a common goal: to allow the people of the city to give witness against the war, while protecting public safety. Toward that end, police and protest leaders agreed to be in constant cell phone contact. Police agreed to let event leaders and peace-keepers be the first line of crowd control, and to intervene only on request of organizers. The result was that in Seattle, over many days, people marched, spoke, sat-in and camped out, without major incident. The Church Council provided peace-keepers, negotiators, sponsored more public events, offered prayer. On Martin Luther King Day, political, community and religious leaders issued a joint covenant to support peaceful relations between people of all races and faiths in our community, drafted and coordinated by the Rev. Jack Olive (Mercer Island United Methodist Church), working with the Mayor's office.

An Outpouring for Peace

As the date grew closer, the tension mounted. It became clear that if war broke out, January 14 might be the last chance for the community to gather in support of peace.

On January 14 the phones and staff at the Church Council were overwhelmed with calls. As the day unfolded, we became aware that the public response would surpass our wildest dreams. When I got in my car at the end of the day to pick up my family and drive to St. James Cathedral, where the event would begin, I reached to turn on the evening news. Just as the sound of the news reached my ears, I quickly turned the radio off again, saying to myself, "For this one night, we will make the news." The traffic was terrible. By the time I reached the Cathedral, people had spilled out into the streets in all directions. In the chaos I arrived late, and had forgotten my clerical robe. Fr. Mike Ryan, in an act of unexpected graciousness, vested me, a Protestant clergy woman, from the sacristy of St. James Cathedral.

We prayed, and we lit our candles, and we sang, and walked: north to Madison, then northeast to Broadway. At Seattle Central Community College, marchers from another direction joined, and we continued north to St. Mark's Cathedral. The city poured out for peace. The crowd numbered 12,000, 30,000 or 60,000, depending on the estimate. The crowd was quiet, determined, hopeful. You could look back down Broadway and see the river of candlelight flowing. Archbishop Hunthausen looked back and quietly said, "Isn't it beautiful?"

Elaine Stanovsky

By March the Gulf War was over, and Seattle, along with every other American city, was busy planning to welcome home the troops. Mayor Rice had a special vision: Seattle would not turn the welcome celebration over to pro-military political conservatives. Seattle would host an event planned by a group with a broad spectrum of opinion about the war: supporters and protesters. Director Stanovsky was invited to participate in the planning. The goal was to find common ground. The goal was to design a celebration in which everyone could participate, supporters as well as critics of the Gulf War. *Operation: Welcome Home* was scheduled for June 22. The planning committee went about its assignment with all seriousness, but in the end there was no common ground, or not enough to support the event. Several members of the committee, including Stanovsky, finally withdrew from the planning group for *Operation: Welcome Home.* Ultimately the event was cancelled because of the controversy.

All the while, a coalition of peace-committed groups had been planning an alternative event, *Walk in the Light,* for the evening of June 21. When the main event was cancelled, *Walk in the Light* remained. It became the community-wide event, with Mayor Norm Rice, many other elected officials, and gubernatorial candidate Mike Lowry, as well as a broad spectrum of religious leaders, including Archbishop Raymond Hunthausen, participating.

Racism: an Undying Legacy

In January, 1991, Elaine Stanovsky met with members of the Baptist Clergy Conference, a colleague group of African-American Baptist clergy. The conversation produced a proposal to pair churches cross-racially for fellowship and shared mission. During the summer of 1991 Saul Michael, an African Methodist Episcopal student from the Interdenominational Theological Center in Atlanta, came to the Church Council as an intern to develop a plan for these pairings. The Parish Partnership Program was launched as a joint project of the Church Council of Greater Seattle and the Black United Clergy for Action in the late fall of 1991. Initially eighteen churches participated, forming nine interracial pairs. These pairings produced: a joint scholarship program (Mercer Island United Methodist and Walker Chapel African Methodist Episcopal), an annual walk for peace and hope on the first Saturday of Advent (Mt. Zion Baptist and Plymouth Congregational, U.C.C.), a focus on education (First African Methodist Episcopal and First Baptist), a choir exchange (Renton First United Methodist and Martin Luther King, Jr. Memorial Baptist) and many other exciting cooperative programs. Bill Grace, of the Center for Ethical Leadership, and colleagues offered training and consultation services for leaders from participating churches about how to work creatively in a multi-cultural context.

On March 12, 1992, the first of a series of Religious Leaders Summit Conferences on Racism was convened at Mt. Zion Baptist Church. Over the next four years four more summits were held, offering a candidates' forum, and opportunities to focus on violence in the community, and the qualities of a healthy community. During these years, many events occurred that challenged the racially diverse community of greater Seattle.

Rodney King Decision—Perhaps the most deeply dividing was the trial of the white police officers who brutalized Rodney King in California. Unrest and violence erupted in communities around the country when the not-guilty verdicts were announced in late spring, 1992. In Seattle Black United Clergy for Action and the Church Council of Greater Seattle jointly sponsored a press conference. Political, business and religious leaders representing a broad spectrum of racial and ethnic heritage gathered to reaffirm their commitment to a just community of multi-racial harmony. On the morning of May 1, leaders from around the region gathered at the Martin Luther King, Jr. Memorial Park. They mucked through wet clay to get near the memorial because the park had never been completed, due to lack of funds. The clay, tracked all over the city on the shoes of Seattle's leaders was a vivid reminder of the unfinished work we have as a nation in healing the wound of racial inequity.

In the fall of 1992 the Council established a Racial Justice Coordinating Committee to guide the work of the Parish Partnership Program, the Summits on Racism, and other initiatives involving racial and ethnic concerns. The committee was staffed first by the Rev. Allen Williams (Walker Chapel African Methodist Episcopal Church) and later by Raymond Miller.

Responding to Arson—By 1996 the nation's attention was focused on what appeared to be a pattern of arson-set fires in African-American churches. Earlier, during the early 1990s, two African-American churches burned in Seattle. Ebenezer African Episcopal Zion Church, the Rev. R. L. Thompson, pastor, was damaged by fire, requiring extensive repairs and renovation. New Hope Baptist Church, pastored by the Rev. Robert Jeffrey was totally destroyed by fire, apparently caused by electrical wiring. Ebenezer was firebombed, though the motive was never clear. The Church Council acted on the conviction that whenever such a tragedy occurred in one of our churches, all the churches should band together in public witness to unity and strength. "Ambassadors" from churches around the region gathered for worship one Sunday with members from Ebenezer in the church basement. Representatives from St. James Cathedral brought their ornate ninety-year-old church banner, and many others were present, giving powerful witness to the unity of the community of faith in moments of hardship. Many churches joined the effort to repair the church. At New Hope, the community gathered outdoors, next to the charred skeleton of the church, to pray, and to promise once again to raise new hope in a community of need and sorrow.

Sexual Abuse and Harassment

In the fall of 1991 the nation sat glued to television coverage of the Senate confirmation hearing for Clarence Thomas, nominated to the Supreme Court of the United States. Anita Hill, his former employee, brought forth allegations that he had sexually harassed her on the job. This highly publicized case opened the eyes of the nation to the dynamics of sexual harassment. Although Thomas was confirmed as a United States Supreme Court Justice, the hearings marked the beginning of a new era. No longer would sexual harassment in the workplace be tolerated.

A related development during the same period involved clergy sexual misconduct. As the world was opening its eyes to sexual harassment in the workplace, the church was opening its eyes to a widespread pattern of clergy sexual abuse of parishioners. One clergy staff person at the Church Council had been forced to resign under allegations of sexual harassment in the workplace during the 1980s.

While ecumenical agencies are not involved in denominational decisions about who is or is not ordained, the broad pattern of clergy sexual abuse affected the Council deeply. During the 1990s, two prominent Seattle pastors were forced to resign from their positions under complaints of sexual involvement with members of their churches. Both had been longstanding, leaders of the Council, and both cases received broad press coverage. These and other similar episodes left deep wounds within the congregations and the ecumenical community.

The Center for the Prevention of Sexual and Domestic Violence, founded by the Rev. Marie Fortune, conducted research and educated the Church about the dynamics and the dangers of clergy sexual abuse. In response to the Center's work, the Church Council gathered a small group of women victims of this abuse for support of one another and of other women who have suffered similarly. The Women's Advocacy Network (WAN) became one place women could turn for guidance in bringing complaints against an offending pastor.

Snoqualmie Falls Preservation

During the early 1990s Puget Power's electrical generation plant at Snoqualmie Falls came due for relicensing by the Federal Energy Regulatory Committee. The plant generates electricity by diverting water above Snoqualmie Falls, running it down long penstock channels within the rock cliff next to the falls, and turning generator turbines with the tremendous force of the water. Puget Power's interest in generating power came into direct conflict with the Snoqualmie Indians' interest in restoring and preserving the falls as an ancient sacred site. The Snoqualmie people, a small tribe not recognized by the federal government, regard the falls as the location of the creation of the world. For generations, many tribes had gathered at the falls to fish and trade. The mist from the mighty falls is understood by the Snoqualmie people to carry prayers to God. When the river is damned and water diverted, the mist is reduced. The sacred power of the falls is compromised by the power production process.

During Puget Power's application for relicensing, the Snoqualmie people began advocating that power generation be discontinued at the falls, and that the site be restored to its original condition. The Native American Task Force of the Church Council of Greater Seattle, under the direction of Ron Adams, joined forces with the tribe, represented by Art Frease, Ron Luzon, and Andy DiAngelo, and other concerned individuals and groups to form the Snoqualmie Falls Preservation Project. This group met with Puget Power and with the media, trying to promote a public use for the falls other than power generation. Building on the foundation of the Native American Apology, signed by church leaders throughout the state of Washington in the 1980s, bishops and regional church executives joined the effort to make the voices of the Snoqualmie people heard in the debate. They met with Puget Power officials, offered leadership at prayer vigils at the falls, and testified at the FERC hearings during the relicensing process. As a result of these efforts, Puget Power dropped all plans to expand the generation facility.

Civil Rights for Sexual Minorities

Public controversy over the rights of gay men, lesbians and bisexuals in society reached a fever pitch during the early 1990s. Following an initiative in the state of Oregon, the Citizen's Alliance of Washington (CAW) was founded for the purpose of limiting and abridging rights of gays and lesbians in the state of Washington. Two citizens' initiatives, 608 and 610, that would have damaged the rights of homosexuals were circulated for signatures in hopes of validating them for the ballot in the fall of 1993. In addition, House Resolution 1449 became the focus of fierce debate. This resolution had been before the State Legislature for many years. It proposed to include gay men, lesbians and bisexuals in the list of groups whose civil rights warranted special protection.

These three legislative controversies led the Church Council to establish the People of Faith for Fairness Task Force. The group offered educational materials and workshops to the churches, and organized a religious community voice in support of increased rights for these sexual minorities. The loudest voices opposing these rights were conservative Christians. It was important for the Church Council, in cooperation with the Washington Association of Churches and other religious groups to speak with a measured, biblically grounded voice in defense of tolerance.

Homelessness

During the 1990s homelessness in greater Seattle and most urban areas in the United States reached crisis proportions. Many factors contributed to the dramatic increase in the number of people living without homes. Mentally ill persons had been moved out of mental institutions during the 1970s and into community-based treatment programs. Over time, funding for these programs decreased and the qualifications for receiving services increased. More and more people in need of services failed to qualify for them. This applied also to drug and alcohol treatment programs, where the wait for residential treatment rose to six months or longer. The combination of these problems with rising housing costs led to growth in the size of the homeless population in King County far beyond the ability of existing shelters and services to respond. As more and more individuals and families came to live in cars, under bridges, and in doorways, the city responded with new, tough measures targeting homeless people.

The Church Council, under the leadership of Urban Minister David Bloom, had been active in advocating and providing services for homeless people since the early 1970s. As the need grew, so did the Council's involvement. In the winter of 1990-91, homeless people and their advocates erected a tent city south of the Kingdome in Seattle, to publicize the plight of the homeless. The Seattle Housing and Resource Effort (SHARE) organized this move, with support from the Seattle Displacement Coalition of the Council, and other homeless advocacy groups. In response to SHARE's concerns, the city of Seattle temporarily turned over an abandoned bus barn near the Seattle Center to the group as a shelter managed by homeless people. Later, the Aloha Motel on Aurora Avenue would be dedicated to self-managed homeless transitional housing as a result of the efforts of SHARE and others.

In 1994 an ordinance was passed by the Seattle City Council making it illegal to sit on the sidewalk on certain streets during business hours, and to urinate in public places. The Seattle Displacement Coalition of the Church Council, staffed by John Fox, sponsored sidewalk sit-ins to protest ordinances targeting homeless people.

Similarly, when the city announced plans to bulldoze a neighborhood of makeshift shacks and tents that had grown up under Interstate 5 on Beacon Hill, the Coalition led an effort to stop the demolition, and to use the event to raise public awareness of the plight of homeless people.

In the early 1990s a broad-based group of citizens and businesses combined efforts to promote a vast city park and redevelopment plan in the Cascade area of downtown, known as the Commons. This plan would have created a "green" corridor from Westlake Center to Lake Union, and promoted the development of commercial and housing projects all along the corridor. The Displacement Coalition organized the few residents of affordable apartments in the area to advocate for the preservation of their homes and neighborhoods and to ensure that the concerns of homeless people were factored into the plan. In due course, the Commons proposal was defeated by the voters.

Homelessness Among Youth—Within the general population of homeless people, a subculture of homeless youth emerged. These young people congregated on Capitol Hill and in the University District. Their circumstances and needs were different from those of other homeless people. The Church Council became involved with homeless youth through the Seattle Displacement Coalition and the Task Force on Housing and Homelessness, directed by Josephine Archuleta. In the University District a partnership developed between the University of Washington, local businesses, homeless service providers and the youth. This group worked cooperatively with the Seattle Police Department to establish good working relationships between police, local businesses and homeless youth, and to offer housing and work opportunities in a supportive community to the youth.

New Ministry Initiatives

Through the many programs of the Church Council, the churches of greater Seattle engaged in vital ministries of justice and mercy from 1990-1995. Education and advocacy continued for a wide range of domestic and international justice and peace concerns. Social services for hungry and homeless people were strengthened and expanded, and significant new programmatic directions were developed.

St. Petersburg-Seattle Sister Churches Program—During the early 1990s communism collapsed in the Soviet Union, and a new, hopeful, though tentative democracy emerged. More and greater exchange between Christians in the United States and the former Soviet Union became possible. The program that began in the 1980s as the Bibles for Leningrad Program (later the Leningrad-Seattle Sister Churches Program) blossomed after *perestroika* into the St. Petersburg-Seattle Sister Churches Program. During the Goodwill Games in the summer of 1990, the choir from the Orthodox Theological Seminary in Leningrad toured the northwest. As part of the tour they offered a joint concert with the St. James Cathedral choir at the cathedral. In May of 1991, Bishop Vincent Warner (Episcopal), led an ecumenical delegation from Seattle to Leningrad. By October, 1991, when a delegation came to Seattle from Russia, Leningrad had once again become St. Petersburg. This delegation, led by Archimandrite Simon, secretary to Metropolitan Iaonn (Russian Orthodox), also included a Roman Catholic, an Evangelical Baptist, a Lutheran and an Armenian Orthodox.

In May, 1992, Bishop Lowell Knudson (ELCA) led another delegation from Seattle, which visited prisons, hospitals, and met with the admiral of the Russian fleet. Cooperation on social ministries and special chaplaincies became the focus of the partnership. Following that exchange, in the fall of 1992, Fr. Boris Besmenov and Dr. Alexander Muzanov came to Seattle for extended consultation and training. Fr. Boris, a professor at the Russian Orthodox Academy in St. Petersburg, had begun a prison chaplaincy program. He studied chaplaincy programs in prisons in the northwest.

Dr. Muzanov was the director of one of the first private hospitals opened after the fall of communism in Russia. St. Xenia's hospital was established in a building on the Academy property under the sponsorship of the Russian Orthodox church. Dr. Muzanov studied with the Sisters of Providence to learn about church medicine in the United States. This visit initiated a new relationship of consultation on church social ministries between our two cities. Other areas of focus included military chaplaincy, drug and alcohol treatment and charitable food distribution. For several years St. Petersburg operated an unprecedented ecumenical coordinating committee for distribution of foreign humanitarian aid.

In 1994, relations with St. Petersburg took another new direction. Attention focused on parish-to-parish partnerships. Churches in the northwest are paired with churches or monastic communities in northwestern Russia for fellowship and mutual support.

Holiday Dinner and Concert—In 1990 David Aasen and June Whitson, volunteers on the development staff, initiated a holiday dinner and concert to benefit the Church Council. The Seattle Men's Chorus, the Northwest Girl Choir, and the Emerald City Chamber

Orchestra offered their gifts of music for the Council. Over the years, the event grew and changed. The Council joined forces with the Multi-Faith AIDS Project of Seattle (MAPS), and under the direction of Louis Magor, the holiday dinner concert became an important annual event honoring religious, political and community leaders and organizations who have supported AIDS awareness and ministry.

Palestinian Concerns Task Force—One of the most important, difficult and painful program initiatives during the early 1990s was the establishment of the Palestinian Concerns Task Force. Board member Dr. Farhat Ziadeh, a Palestinian and professor emeritus at the University of Washington, saw the need for such a task force and initiated discussions to form one. Unfortunately, representatives of the Jewish community perceived this effort as hostile to hopes for peace in the Middle East. After a year of painstaking deliberations and attempts at consensus building and conflict resolution between the conflicted groups, the Board of Directors authorized the creation of the Palestinian Concerns Task Force in the fall of 1994. The first activity of the Task Force was to sponsor a Palestine Awareness week in November of 1994. Both the decision of the Church Council to authorize the Task Force and the promotional materials developed for the week inflamed some leaders in the Jewish community. Support for the Jewish-Christian Task Force of the Church Council was withdrawn and it became inactive at this time. An alternative committee was begun under the auspices of the American Jewish Committee to continue the work of Jewish-Christian relations, free from the fear of betrayal by the Church Council. Even as peace seemed hopeful in the Middle East, it was unattainable for people of faith in greater Seattle.

Children, Youth and Families—The early 1990s saw the Family Life Task Force transformed into the Task Force on Children, Youth and Families, with new energy and focus. This Task Force sponsored a community-wide conference called "Welcome the Children" in February, 1993, and launched an ambitious program offering seed grants to programs working with youth. In addition, it became a major promoter of the Virtues Project in the Seattle area. The Virtues Project trained adults who work with children to teach them fifty-two classical virtues from the religious traditions of the world as guides and resources for life. Developed by Linda Popov, the virtues curriculum focuses on encouraging children's spiritual development alongside their intellectual and physical development. The non-sectarian approach was widely appreciated by many parents and teachers who participated in several workshops over a number of years.

The Ecumenical Program for Urban Service (EPRUS)—The work of the Children, Youth and Families Task Force also gave rise to an important, broad-reaching programmatic initiative in the Council. In 1994 the Federal Government initiated the AmeriCorps program of voluntary service, reminiscent of both the Conservation Corps and VISTA. Under the umbrella of the National Council of the Churches of Christ, the Church Council of Greater Seattle joined with four other ecumenical councils around the country in the Ecumenical Program for Urban Service (EPRUS) to receive funding as an AmeriCorps project. In Seattle, Terryl Ross directed the program, under the supervision of David Bloom. Twenty-five volunteers served through EPRUS in Seattle, carrying out the theme of "Making Connections for Children and Youth." They staffed after-school programs, worked with homeless youth, initiated the Youth Garden Works which trained and employed homeless youth, and supported the work of the Youth Chaplaincy Program at the detention center.

Music and the Arts Ministry—George Shangrow, founding conductor of Orchestra Seattle and host of KING-FM's "Live by George," launched the Church Council's new Music and the Arts Task Force by organizing an Ecumenical Choir. The original forty voices represented a wide range of religious communities: Roman Catholic, Disciples of Christ, United Church of Christ, Lutheran, United Methodist, Presbyterian, Quaker, Unitarian Universalist and Unity. In June, 1995, the group gave its first performance, the Fauré *Requiem*.

Milestones: Events, Retirements, Esteemed Visitors

O. J. Moore Retires—The Rev. O. J. Moore, founding director of the Emergency Feeding Program retired in 1990 after fourteen years of ministry to the hungry. He was succeeded by Arthur Lee. This program was an important cooperative effort of the Church Council of Greater Seattle and the Black United Clergy for Action.

Archbishop Hunthausen Retires—In the fall of 1991, Archbishop Hunthausen, beloved leader of the Archdiocese of Seattle and outspoken advocate for peace and disarmament, retired after sixteen years in Seattle. He was succeeded by Archbishop Thomas Murphy.

Greek Orthodox Join the Council—At the Annual Meeting of the Church Council in May, 1992, an application for membership from the Greek Orthodox Church was approved. The Annual Meeting in 1995 was hosted by Fr. Steve Tsiclis and the Church of the Assumption, with Fr. Leonid Kishkovsky of the Orthodox Church in America (Russian-American) offering the keynote address.

Archbishop of Canterbury Visits—The Archbishop of Canterbury, George Carey, and his wife, Mrs. Eileen Carey visited Seattle in September, 1992. Meeting with the ecumenical bishops and denominational executives group in Seattle, he commented on the fact that the individuals in the group know one another and are at ease with one another. In other cities he visited in the United States, church officials seemed to be meeting one another for the first time on the occasion of his visit.

Observance of the 500th Anniversary of Columbus' Arrival in America—While many in the United States and Europe celebrated the 500th anniversary of the "discovery of America," the Church Council encouraged sober observation of the anniversary, recalling the ancient peoples who had lived here countless centuries before visitors from Europe arrived. Through the Native American Task Force, educational materials were distributed which honored the first peoples of this land, and invited gratitude and humility on the part of European "newcomers."

The Dalai Lama Visits Seattle—His Holiness XIVth Dalai Lama of Tibet visited Seattle in June 1993. As part of his visit an interfaith worship service was held at St. Mark's Cathedral, co-sponsored by St. Mark's and the Interfaith Council of Washington State.

The Presses Stopped—When Lyndol Pullen retired after a long and distinguished career as press operator at the Church Council at the end of 1993, the presses stopped rolling. Russian Orthodox Metropolitan Alexsiy from Leningrad had been very impressed by the print room when he visited the Council offices on his trip to celebrate the millennium of Christianity in Russia. His reaction reminded everyone of the importance of the printed word to the creation of a free and informed public. An era ended when the Council lost its printing capability.

End of Apartheid in South Africa—South Africa held its first free, racially participatory elections in April, 1994. The Church Council had advocated, educated and protested for an end to apartheid through its Task Force on Southern Africa. As a result of the Task Force's tireless efforts, Marjorie Prince, longtime chair, was invited to be part of the Ecumenical Monitoring Programme in South Africa (EMPSA) for the elections. The Council celebrated with people of color in South Africa the end of apartheid and the election of Nelson Mandela as president of a new free South Africa.

Dedication of Remodeled St. James Cathedral—During 1994 St. James Cathedral underwent significant architectural redesign, moving the high altar to the center of the cruciform nave. The Cathedral reopened on Christmas Eve, 1994, and a series of rededication events went on for weeks following. Among them was the Week of Prayer for Christian Unity celebration, co-sponsored by the Cathedral and the Church Council of Greater Seattle.

Farmworkers—After eight years of organizing and boycotting, the Ste. Michelle winery finally reached an agreement with farmworkers to hold union elections in June of 1995. The Church Council Farmworkers Support Task Force helped promote the boycott of Ste. Michelle products in the Seattle area.

In Conclusion

In 1995 the Church Council turned its sights toward the year 2000. It looked forward to the leadership of its new president-director, the Rev. Tom Quigley, at a time when ecumenical agencies were said to be in crisis. But crisis is a time of "opportunity and danger where identity, purpose and vitality are at stake," writes Gary Peluso, a researcher for the Lilly Endowment. ("The Crisis of Local and Regional Ecumenism," *Midstream: the Ecumenical Movement Today*, vol. 32, no. 4, October, 1993.) All across the nation regional and local ecumenical agencies seemed to be in such a crisis. But in greater Seattle, the ecumenical community has learned to weather change and even crisis. The Church Council of Greater Seattle learned that it could survive a change in directors. Its witness and ministry remained vital through the transition. Its component parts began to keep the health and welfare of the whole Council in view, even as they focused their energy on their specific purpose. Its Board of Directors entered into a process of examining and changing the Council in order to improve the quality of its life and work.

Through this period the Council thrived because people of passion and vision worked sacrificially to keep it vital. The remarkable commitment of the core staff over many years of service is testimony to the vitality of the mission: Alice Woldt, David Bloom, Angela Ford, Joy Estille, Anne Porter, Pat Watts, Carol Sue Elliot, Lyndol Pullen, and Marge Lueders. In addition, scores of creative, zealous program staff took the Council into the community in myriad forms. Vice Presidents Laura Bailey, the Rev. Rodney Romney and Joan Merritt were sources of wisdom and stability. Literally hundreds of individuals enlivened the Church Council through their volunteer hours and financial contributions.

The challenges ahead are continuous with the challenges of the past. More and more people need services that they cannot afford; fewer and fewer jobs pay a living wage; children and youth are embracing violence as a way of life; racially-based distrust and hatred are increasing even as our nation becomes more and more racially diverse; more and more people are drifting through life outside any secure, stable community of support and companionship.

So long as the conditions of the natural and the social world fall short of God's promises, Christians will experience an irresistible lure into ministries of justice and mercy. So long as there are walls dividing people from one another, Christians will experience an undeniable urge to reach across the barriers to create community.

The Church Council of Greater Seattle continues to be a place of connection and adventure, attracting people who see an opportunity in every crisis. It is characterized by spontaneity and diversity. Its challenge, always, is to direct its energies and passions effectively. Through times of glory and vilification, in the midst of the struggle that living water flows. Over and over again, lives are touched and changed, a prophetic word is heard, abuse of power is challenged, community is built, sorrow and sighing flee away.

Epilogue

In the mid-1990s, the Board of Directors of the Church Council of Greater Seattle held a retreat to assess directions and plan for the future. In the course of the retreat each participant was asked to suggest an image or object as a metaphor for the life and work of the Council. Many fine images were suggested, but the one that remains with me, and which has been reaffirmed as I have read this remarkable history, is that of a river.

The river is a strong symbol in sacred literature. The Hebrew scriptures begin by describing a river that flows out of Eden to water the garden, before it divides into four rivers (*Genesis 2*). The Christian scriptures end with the image of a river of the water of life, bright as crystal, flowing from the throne of God for the healing of the nations (*Revelation 22*).

As I have sifted through the words that have been assembled to preserve the history of an ecumenical organization I have come to love, I am reminded of a river making its way through a city, gathering force as it flows, offering healing and life to all. On a few occasions the river is reduced to a trickle, either through lack of financial support or lack of grassroots participation and vision. But always it regains momentum, sometimes creating tributaries and confluences, before returning to the one stream that symbolizes the yearning need of all humans to be one.

Through the tireless efforts of the Rev. Gertrude Apel, the nurturing guidance of the Rev. Lemuel Petersen, the courageous example of Dr. William Cate, the articulate skill of the Rev. Elaine Stanovsky, the visionary experience of the Rev. Thomas Quigley, and the energetic support of thousands not named here, the Council river is now wending its way towards a century of faithful witness. The future of that river belongs to those of us who read this story and claim part of it as our own.

I can think of no period of history when it could have been more significant to be a member of Christian koinonia and interfaith partnership than now. It is possible at this juncture in time, after centuries of self-seeking and self-deception, the Church is ready to believe in the Bible's own picture of it, a river flowing from the throne of God to bring healing to all the nations. In all the disturbing turbulence of World War II and the Vietnam War, through the Civil Rights movement and the discrimination against minorities and women, fighting the constant battle of human rights for all people, the Church Council has faithfully tried to heal some of the brokenness in our communities, to increase justice for marginal people, and to help build a world of peace, justice and well-being for all.

Perhaps like the legendary Siddhartha we must all come to a river where we hear a unique sound, the sound that signals the true beginning of life and the discovery that love is the most important thing in the world. When we make that discovery, we are then ready to serve the world in the name of the One who, in love, has invited us to be guests on this beautiful planet at this crucial time in human history.

Rodney Romney
Pastor, Seattle First Baptist Church

About the Authors

Jessie Kinnear Kenton was Youth Director at Boulevard Park Presbyterian Church in Seattle for seven years. Beginning ecumenical work in 1960 with the old Council of Churches of Greater Seattle, she remained in that position for ten years. With the founding of the Church Council of Greater Seattle in 1970, she continued as Executive Administrator working in finance and program development.

Jessie was the first woman to receive her Fellow in Church Business Administration (FCBA) in 1963. She received her BA in Business Management and Commu-

Jessie Kinnear Kenton

nity Development in 1977 from Western Washington University in Bellingham, Washington. This was fifty years after her graduation from high school. She completed work in 1985 for an MA in Education for Values, from the San Francisco Theological Seminary in California. Her thesis topic was "Changing Values in Ecumenical Strategy in the Greater Seattle Area—1919 to 1984."

The founder of many ecumenical ventures, including The Coalition on Women and Religion (1973), *The Source*, an award-winning ecumenical newspaper in Seattle (1978), the Women's Credit Union, the Girl's Club of Puget Sound, and New Beginnings, a shelter for battered women and children (1976), she has encouraged women to serve on boards and committees. She was an officer of the Renton Ecumenical Association of Churches (REACH) from 1986 to 1991.

Long active in volunteer work, Jessie continues teaching, volunteer work and her writing at Panorama City, a retirement community in Lacey, Washington, where she resides. She has organized PanPress, to help other writers in publishing their books.

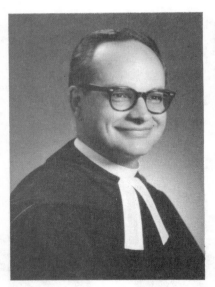

Lemuel Alva Petersen

Along the way Lem Petersen has had a considerable variety of professional experiences. He has been a newspaperman, writer, editor, junior college teacher, publicist and public relations director, non-profit fund-raiser, local church minister, ecumenical administrator, community organizer, physical planning and low-income housing coordinator, and government personnel specialist.

Early professional affiliations included the International Council of Religious Education, National Council of Churches, Church Federation of Greater Chicago, and National Conference of Christians and Jews—in Chicago and New York City—as well Hyde Park Union Church in Chicago. He served as Executive Minister for the Council of Churches of Greater Seattle from January 1, 1959, to June 1, 1968.

Until March 1971, he worked for the City of Seattle in its Model City Program as Physical Environment and Housing Planning Coordinator. Between 1971 and 1987 he was in personnel work, mostly with Seattle's Department of Community Development.

With degrees from the University of Minnesota (1943) and Yale University Divinity School (1947), Dr. Petersen has done additional graduate work at Northwestern University, University of Chicago, Chicago Theological Seminary, and University of Washington.

He was ordained in an American Baptist church (1947), but for many years has also been a member of Congregational and United Church of Christ congregations (where he now holds his clergy standing). In 1961 he was awarded an honorary doctor of divinity degree from Presbyterian-related Whitworth College, of Spokane.

He has enjoyed a marriage of 52 years with Melba Runtz Petersen, and has been blessed with a daughter, Helsa, and a grandson, Devin.

William B. Cate was President-Director of the Church Council of Greater Seattle from 1970 to 1990. Prior to that he served for five years as executive of the Interchurch Council of Greater New Bedford, Massachusetts, 1953 to 1958, and twelve years as executive of the Greater Portland, Oregon, Council of Churches, 1958 to 1970. His undergraduate education was at Willamette University. At Boston University, he earned a Bachelor of Sacred Theology degree in 1948 and a Ph.D in Social Ethics in 1953. His dissertation was entitled

William B. Cate

"Practical and Theoretical Aspects of Ecumenical Communication." He also studied in 1950 at the Ecumenical Institute of the World Council of Churches near Geneva, Switzerland and at the University of Basel in Basel, Switzerland.

Dr. Cate has written many articles and chapters in books on ecumenism over the years. He is author of two books: *The Ecumenical Scandal on Main Street*, 1965, and *The One Church in this Place*, 1991.

Born in Texas in 1924 and reared in Idaho, he married Janice Patterson in 1946. They have six children and twelve grandchildren. Dr. Cate was ordained an elder in the United Methodist Church in 1952 and has served most of his active ministry in conciliar leadership. He retired from the Pacific Northwest Conference of the United Methodist Church in June 1990.

He served as a vice-president of the National Council of Churches in the 1970s and president of the National Association of Ecumenical Staff in 1971-1972. In 1965 he received an honorary Doctor of Divinity degree from Lewis and Clark University in Portland, Oregon.

174

Elaine J. W. Stanovsky

Elaine J.W. Stanovsky is currently the Puget Sound District Superintendent for the United Methodist Church. A lifelong resident of western Washington, she earned her BA in 1976 from the University of Puget Sound, and her MDiv from Harvard Divinity School in 1981. Ordained in the United Methodist Church in 1983, she served as pastor of the Kennydale United Methodist Church in Renton, WA, from 1981 to 1988, and of Crown Hill United Methodist Church in Seattle from 1988 to 1990. Her interest in ecumenical affairs dates back to 1976, when she became involved in the Consultation on Church Union. As President-Director of the Church Council of Greater Seattle from 1990-1995, she made two trips to St. Petersburg, Russia, with the Sister Churches delegation, and attended the World Council of Churches General Assembly in Canberra, Australia, in 1991.

Her leadership of the Church Council was marked by significant initiatives in the area of Christian witness for peace, the nurturing of meaningful partnerships between Christians of different ethnicity, race and nationality, creative programming to address the complex problems facing contemporary families and children, and continuing efforts to achieve justice for the disadvantaged in our society.

She is an Honorary Board Member of the Northwest AIDS Foundation and a Trustee of the University of Puget Sound. She also serves on the Advisory Board of the People's Memorial Association and on the Board of Directors of the Deaconess Children's Service in Everett, WA.

She and her husband, Clint, have three sons.

Index

A

Aasen, David, 99, 147,151,163
Adams, John Hurst, 39, 47, 62
Adams, Ronald,143,159
Ahmed, Ismail, 102
Aleksiy, Metropolitan, 96,142,166
Allen, Steve,112,147
Allende, Salvadore, 85
American Bible Society, 34
American Indian Women's Service
  League, 59
Anderson, Marion, 121
Anderson, Peter, 141
Angle, Grant, 99
Apartheid in South Africa, 85, 123
Apel, Gertrude Louise,10,13,18,21,
  26,30,87,89,170
Arafat, Yassir, 137
Archbishop of Canterbury, 166
Archeluda, Josephine, 101,162
Armed Services, 20,54

B

Bader, Diana, 105,149
Bailey, Ambrose, 5
Bailey, Laura, 149,168
Baird, Lucius, 5,10
Barnes, Roswell P., 66
Barnett, Arthur, 19
Bauck, Steve, 126
Bayley, Frank S., 2
Bayne, Stephen, 53
Beck, Mary Lou, 83
Beeman, Paul, 39
Beginning
  Ecumenical Work, 4
Frontier Churches, 3,4
Home Missions, 1,2
International, 1
Ministerial Associations, 2
N.Y. Federation, 1
Bellah, Robert,120
Berry, Michael, 116
Bhaskarananda, Swami, 145
Bible as Literature, The court
  case, 62
Bibles for Leningrad, 141
Bicentennial Celebration, 145
Black Dollar Days, 82
Black United Clergy for Action,
  83,165
Bliss, W.H.,5
Bloom, David, 98,126,127, 141,
  148,165,168
Bode, Theodore, 81
Boeing Employment, 76,79
Boeing Company, 76,112
Boldt, George, 86
Bollen, M.E., 5
Boonstra, John, 123
Bostrom, E.W., 34
Boulding, Elise, 120
Bowman, Eva, 27
Boycotts, grape and others,
  107,123,125
Braman, Dorm, 31
Brauer, Jerald C., 65
Bryant, Anita, 104,105
Buerge, David, 145
Bundy, Emory, 79,82,140
Burgess, H.F., 2
Bush, Ann Williams, 110
Bushnell, Helen, 8
Byrd, Richard, 17

175

K

Kennedy, John F., Pres., 36,53
King County, 28,31
King, H.R., 5,7
King, Martin Luther, Jr. 41
King, Rodney, 157
Kinnear (Kenton), Jessie, 1,10,11,
  19,24,59,73,79,105,114,140,171
Kishkovsky, Leonid, 166
Kleihauer, Cleveland, 5
Knutson, Lowell, 141
Kramer, A.L., 55
Kring, Mr. And Mrs. Soren, 27
Kruzner, Donald, 25
Kuhn, A.O., 2
Kuyper, Neal, 58

L

La France, Joan, 86
Langford, Victor, 129
Lay School of Theology, 63
Laytner, Anson, 145
Lazenby, Herbert, 64
Lee, Arthur, 93,165
Leningrad/Seattle Sister City, 141
Lenoir, George, 125
Levine, Raphael, 42
Liberation Theology, 134
Lintner, Jay, 112,120
Littell, Franklin H., 120
Living Room Dialogue, 43
Local Churches Divest, 124
Loomis, Hazel, 6
Lowry, Mike, Gov., 156
Luce, F.H., 5
Lueders, Marge, 99,114,168
Luke, Wing, 31,55
Luzon, Ron, 159
Lynch, Jack, 36,38

M

M.L.K. Memorial Park, 157
Mackey, Sally, 149
Macrae, Marjorie, 27
Magee, John B., 18

Magnuson, Jon, 142,143
Malonson, Ray, 108
Marcos, Ferdinand, Imelda, 135
Martin, Joe, 98,109
Marty, Martin, 141
Matthews, Mark A., 5,8
May, Charles, 133
Maze, Peggy, 83
McCleave, George, 58,107
McConkey, Paul, 20
McElheran, Pearl, 104
McHenry, Ward, 2
McKinney, Samuel B., 36,39,72,
  91,100
Meade, Christine, 54
Meconis, Charles, 94,120,121
Mental Health, 109,132
Mergers, 11,12,14,114
Merritt, Joan, 168
METRO, 32
Michael, R.H., 5
Michael, Saul, 156
Middle East, 154
Migrant ministry, 59,60
Miller, B. Franklin, 37
Miller, Randolph Crump, 43
Miller, Raymond, 157
Minority employment, 37
Mirel, James, 145
Mitchell, John (Jack), 44,149
Mitchell, Ed, 61
Mohajer-Jasbi, Pasha, 45
Mook, Charles, 5
Moore, Otis J., 83,165
Morgan, Max W., 72
Murphy, U G., 5
Murphy, Thomas, 166
Murray, Cecil B., 118
Music and Arts, 165

N

NAACP, 38,119
Nakayama, Timothy,
  92,116,135,136,149
Native Americans, 85,86,142
Neighbors in Need, 80,82
Nelson, Jonathan, 94,122

Nelson, Ruth Youngdahl, 122
New Ecumenical Creation
  Issues, 77
  Values, 80
New Hope Church Arson Fire,
  157
New Interfaith Developments,
  112,139
Norcross, D.E., 20
North Ireland Crisis, 110
Northup, Frederick, 102
Nuclear Energy ,120,121
Nursing homes, 58

O

Odegaard, Charles, 62
Official Observers/interfaith
  partners, 25,112
Olive, Jack, 154
Olsen, Andrea, 26,27,60,89
One Church in This Place, 173
Open Housing, 35,39
Operation Welcome Home, 156
Organization of Labor Unions,
  41,82,107,130,131
Orrill, R.N., 5
Ortman, David, 120
Ostrander, Clinton, 23
Overseas Relief, 60

P

Pacific Rim Immigrants, 112,136
Palestine Concerns, 84,137,164
Palmer, Everett, 90
Parish Partnership Plan, 156
Parish to Parish Partnerships,
  Russia, 163
Parker, Bruce, 103
Parlin, Charles, 66
Pastoral care, 57,109
Peace and Justice, 15,115
Peace—South Africa, 85,124,125
Peace—Vietnam, Chilean
  Refugees, 84
Pelton, Gerald, 27
Peluso, Gary, 167

People of Faith/Fairness Task
  Force, 160
Perry, Harold (Hal), 80
Petersen, Lemuel A.,
  30,31,51,56,91,170,172
Petersen, Melba, 33,172
Phillips, Bettie, 59,73
Pickering, Joe, 109
Pinochet, August, 85
Polhemus, Clarence E., 87
Pope John XXIII, 41
Popov, Linda, 164
Porter, Anne, 168
Praying Wolf James, Jewel, 142
Presbyterian Counseling
  Service, 58
Preservation of Religious objects,
  43,158
Pretlow, R.E., 5
Prince, Marjorie ,126,167
Protestant Building, 23,71
Pruitt, Kathleen, 102
Public Affairs, 54
Pullen, Lyndol, 99,166,168

Q

Quigley, Thomas, 167,190

R

Racial Equality, 25,181
Racial Justice, 80
Raible, Peter, 112,136,145
Ramsay, Chester, 27,89
Raver, Paul, 72
Reagan, Ronald, Pres., 129
Redesign of the Council, 41,45,47
Redlining, 115,116
Reed, Joan, 99,114
Religion, Drama, Arts, 146
Religious Leaders Summit, 157
Rennebohm, Craig, 109,132
Rice, Norman, Mayor, 100,154-
  156
Ricker, Maude, 56,73
Ridenour, C.M. ,19
Rieke, Luvern V., 34